SOCIAL MEDIA FOR STUDENT AFFAIRS IN #HIGHEREDUCATION

SOCIAL MEDIA FOR STUDENT AFFAIRS IN #HIGHEREDUCATION

Trends, Challenges, and Opportunities

Brandon C. Waite
Darren A. Wheeler

ROWMAN & LITTLEFIELD
Lanham • Boulder • New York • London

Published by Rowman & Littlefield
An imprint of The Rowman & Littlefield Publishing Group, Inc.
4501 Forbes Boulevard, Suite 200, Lanham, Maryland 20706
www.rowman.com

6 Tinworth Street, London SE11 5AL

Copyright © 2020 by Brandon C. Waite and Darren A. Wheeler

All rights reserved. No part of this book may be reproduced in any form or by any electronic or mechanical means, including information storage and retrieval systems, without written permission from the publisher, except by a reviewer who may quote passages in a review.

British Library Cataloguing in Publication Information Available

Library of Congress Cataloging-in-Publication Data

Names: Waite, Brandon C., author. | Wheeler, Darren A., author.
Title: Social media for student affairs in #highereducation : trends, challenges, and opportunities / Brandon C. Waite, Darren A. Wheeler. Other titles: Social media for student affairs in hashtag higher education.
Description: Lanham : Rowman & Littlefield, [2020] | Includes bibliographical references and index. | Summary: "This book explores the ways student affairs professionals in higher education use social media as a new tool to help them accomplish their goals on campus"—Provided by publisher.
Identifiers: LCCN 2019043432 (print) | LCCN 2019043433 (ebook) | ISBN 9781475845747 (cloth) | ISBN 9781475845754 (paperback) | ISBN 9781475845761 (epub)
Subjects: LCSH: Student affairs services—Administration. | Social media in education. | Education, Higher—Effect of technological innovations on.
Classification: LCC LB2342.9 .W35 2020 (print) | LCC LB2342.9 (ebook) | DDC 378.1/97—dc23
LC record available at https://lccn.loc.gov/2019043432
LC ebook record available at https://lccn.loc.gov/2019043433

To Oslo and Sigrid and Amy

CONTENTS

Preface ix
Acknowledgments xi
Introduction xiii

1. Social Media Strategies for Recruitment, Admissions, and Enrollment 1
2. Social Media Strategies in Academic Services 27
3. Social Media Strategies for Student Health and Wellness 55
4. Social Media Strategies for Campus Safety 73
5. Social Media Strategies for Career and Alumni Services 91

Conclusion 111
Bibliography 117
About the Authors 131

PREFACE

We have spent more than a decade teaching political science at Ball State University. During this time, we have worked alongside student affairs professionals to address a wide range of issues related to recruitment and retention, advising and mentoring, student health and wellness, campus safety and security, career planning and job market preparation, and alumni relations. We have witnessed how the rise of social media has resulted in new opportunities and challenges related to each of these key areas of student affairs.

Unfortunately, we have also observed a dearth of academic literature regarding topics related to social media and these various facets of student affairs. Higher-education professionals are largely left to figure out social media on their own, which can be a daunting task given their other job responsibilities. The purpose of this book is to fill this void in the literature by giving the topic of social media in student affairs the comprehensive examination it deserves. We hope this book helps higher-education professionals, particularly those who work in student affairs, better understand and make use of these new media technologies in their daily routines.

ACKNOWLEDGMENTS

We are grateful to all the students, parents, and student affairs professionals who took the time to discuss the subject matter of this book with us. Their insights, stories, and opinions were invaluable. We would also like to thank Rowman & Littlefield for having the confidence in us to complete this project. It has been a pleasure working with our acquisitions editor, Sarah Jubar. We are fortunate that Ball State University and the Department of Political Science supported our efforts with course release time for research and a well-timed sabbatical that allowed for the completion of this book in a timely fashion. Finally, we are grateful to our families for the sacrifices they made and the encouragement they provided while we worked on this project.

INTRODUCTION

The pace of technological change can often seem relentless. The rise of personal computing, the Internet, smartphones, and social media applications occurred in a relatively short time frame and have affected nearly every facet of society. Colleges and universities are not immune to these trends, and somewhat paradoxically they often find themselves both ahead of and behind the technological curve.

These institutions are typically populated by young adults adept at using the latest gadgets and applications, but higher education is also steeped in tradition, so universities often trail their business counterparts when it comes to effectively integrating new technologies into their daily operations. This keeps institutions from squandering resources chasing every new fad, but it can pose problems given that colleges and universities need to market their ability to meet the needs of today's students in a modern setting with cutting-edge resources and processes.

The impact that technology has had on college campuses is a phenomenon that has received considerable attention. The birth of online classes and increased use of technology in the classroom has spawned a considerable literature that explores how technology, the Internet, and social media affect the way professors teach and students learn.[1] Others have explored how social media can be used to build student communities outside the classroom,[2] or how academic departments use social media to accomplish their goals.[3] However, there is far less research that explores how technology—and in particular social media platforms such as Facebook, Twitter, Instagram, and YouTube—is changing the face of student affairs.[4]

This book takes a substantial step toward filling this gap in the literature. Each chapter explores a different dimension of student affairs, providing an overview of key challenges and discussing the ways that social media tools can contribute to or mitigate them. By providing specific examples and thought-provoking questions, this book helps higher-education professionals gain the capacity to develop creative social media solutions that are appropriate for their own situations as they seek to strategically integrate these technologies into their daily regime.

Research in this area is important for a variety of reasons. Student affairs professionals are responsible for a wide range of tasks and services that are directly related to student success, and thus the success of the institution. Like their counterparts across campus, student affairs units are increasingly being asked to do more with less. This means they are exploring new, more efficient means of accomplishing their goals. This book will help them do so by taking a thoughtful, systematic approach to understanding social media, the problems it can cause, and the means by which it can be used to help students develop the skills necessary for self-advocacy and self-determination.

STUDENT AFFAIRS

The area known today as "student affairs" has variously been referred to as "student personnel," "student services," or "student development" over the years.[5] Its existence flows from the idea that there is more to educating a student than what goes on in the classroom. Students are people with social, emotional, and spiritual needs. Students cannot learn if they are sick, or are having trouble finding appropriate housing, or are in doubt about which classes to take, or are finding it difficult to make friends. These issues should be addressed not just for their own sake but because addressing them helps facilitate student learning. Student affairs plays a vital role in the holistic approach to educating students.[6]

Colleges and universities in the United States were originally founded and organized in part upon the concept of *in loco parentis*. The institution—usually via its professors and the university president—was responsible for the educational, spiritual, and moral well-being of those students entrusted to its care. Students lived in dormitories, and discipline was often strict.[7] This approach began to change somewhat after the Civil War as professors became more focused on teaching and research and less on the nonacademic aspects of their students' lives.

In the 1920s, the first administrators—deans of men (later to become deans of students)—began to appear on campus. Their purpose was to enforce college and university rules. Physicians also began to appear on campuses at about this time, followed shortly by personnel whose responsibility it was to monitor records and provide advising and vocational guidance.[8] As student affairs personnel began to proliferate on campus, the influential *Student Personnel Point of View* was published in 1937. This was the first significant discipline-wide attempt to articulate what student affairs personnel did and why it was important.[9] An updated version of this important work was issued in 1949.[10]

The latter half of the twentieth century on campus saw a change in both the number of students on campus and how they interacted with university personnel. There was a tremendous explosion in the number of people who attended college following World War II. Among these were veterans attending on the new G.I. Bill. This era also saw an increase in minority and first-generation college students. This influx of new student populations combined with the social and political turmoil of the 1960s and the Vietnam War often made college campuses a flashpoint for conflict.

During this time, expectations regarding the ways in which college students were supposed to interact and coexist with authority changed. New theories were espoused explaining the relationship between individual characteristics, the learning environment, and student outcomes. This paved the way for the advent of additional services on campuses, particularly for underrepresented populations.[11]

Student affairs has grown astronomically in recent decades and now covers a considerable number of areas, including admissions, advising, career services, campus ministries, campus safety, computer services, disability services, Greek affairs, health/counseling services, housing/residential life, judicial affairs, orientation programs, multicultural student services, recreation and fitness, student activities, student unions/centers, and alumni affairs.[12] Adding to the complexity is the fact that the number of online students—who may never set foot on campus—is increasing. Student affairs personnel must serve this population and its unique needs as well.

Student affairs researchers have primarily focused on four areas: the categories of people/jobs that fall under student affairs, the type of work that student affairs workers have done over time, the skills and abilities needed for student affairs workers to perform their jobs, and the characteristics of the student affairs labor pool (primarily in regard to the problem of attrition).[13] To the degree that technology is discussed in the context of student affairs, it usually occurs under the rubric of skills/abilities needed by student affairs professionals. Even then, academic coverage of these issues has been sporadic and incomplete. This book helps remedy that problem.

STUDENT AFFAIRS AND TECHNOLOGY ON CAMPUS

The emergence of technology in student affairs has occurred in three waves, each of which has been accompanied by new challenges and opportunities. These changes in technology have, in some ways, fundamentally changed the nature of the relationship between student affairs professionals and college students. Understanding these changes is key to solving today's most pressing problems in higher education.

The first wave involved the birth and widespread use of the personal computer (e.g., a computer that sits on an employee's desk). Early campus computers were large mainframes. Not everyone had access to them, and they were often difficult to use. Personal computers decentralized the power of computing, paving the way for their regular and widespread use. At a very basic level, employees could now conduct word processing and store data more easily than ever, resulting in considerable time savings. As software became more advanced and targeted to specific areas (e.g., inventory management software for campus libraries or registration tracking software for admissions and the Registrar's Office), personal computers became even more useful.

In the 1980s, there was some resistance to technological change in campus offices for a variety of reasons. There was initially a lack of funding for technology, it was difficult to keep staff appropriately trained, and there was some apprehensiveness on the part of staff to embrace poorly understood tools.[14] In 1990, one scholar noted that, historically, there had been "little mention of technology in the student affairs literature."[15]

Despite this, a 1991 survey of student affairs professionals identified computers as the solution to many of their most frequently mentioned problems.[16] This is because computer technology has the capacity to complete any number of tasks more quickly, freeing student affairs professionals for more one-on-one time with students.[17] As the 1990s progressed, computer technologies became increasingly important to the "high-touch" strategies employed by student affairs professionals.

The next transformational wave occurred as a result of the rise of the Internet and World Wide Web. These online technologies allowed people and organizations to share information with each other at previously unfathomable rates. By 1997, 84 percent of those in student affairs were using email on a daily basis.[18] Communication became instantaneous. Students were driven to university and department web pages full of information. These pages originally contained static content, essentially printed brochure-type material. Over time, students also gained the ability to engage in transactional behavior such as filling out forms to pay bills, order services, or register for classes. University websites eventually became advanced enough to offer student portals that provided students with individualized, personal information.[19]

Student affairs professionals recognized these trends, and by 2010, the American College Professional Association (ACPA) articulated the importance of technology in student affairs by adding it to their list of core competency areas. "Technology," the ACPA document reads, "focuses on the use of digital tools, resources, and technologies for the advancement of student learning, development, and success."[20] The question is not how technology will replace the "high-touch" methods that have been at the heart of student affairs since its inception but rather how new tools can be used to supplement these methods in order to produce an even more effective, more personal student affairs experience for college students.

The most recent technological wave to hit higher education involves the rise of social media. This stage focuses on real-time interaction and a high degree of personalization. One scholar referred to it as the "mass customization of learning."[21] Sometimes described as Web 2.0, social media share an interactive component that differentiates them from the one-way content-driven models conceived in the early life of the Internet. Social media can include various types of technologies, including online forums (e.g., Reddit), blogs (e.g., WordPress), social networking sites (e.g., Facebook), social bookmarking sites (e.g., Pinterest), video sharing sites (e.g., YouTube), photo sharing sites (e.g., Flickr, Instagram), streaming sites (e.g., Ustream), user reviews (e.g., Yelp), crowdsourcing (e.g., Wikipedia), and content aggregators (e.g., Hootsuite). Smartphone and web-based applications can also have interactive components that are characteristic of Web 2.0 technologies.

As will become clear in the following chapters, the relationship between social media and student affairs is complex. These technologies affect how students view themselves and their surroundings, which is often reflected in their carefully crafted digital identities, or the way they interact with their peers, professors, and student affairs personnel. Social media may be contributing to the number and nature of problems faced by students.

At the same time, these online platforms can provide student affairs professionals with new means of overcoming the challenges associated with key tasks. This may involve student affairs personnel acting as a broker to third-party social media platforms, simply directing students to them and then assisting them if, or when, students request. At other times, student affairs professionals use social media to directly reach and interact with students. Student affairs professionals who lack the technological capacity to understand and use these tools appropriately are finding it increasingly difficult to do their job well.

Student affairs professionals are constantly bombarded with the admonition of how important it is to become "tech literate" and keep current with the latest devices and software, but as the examples in this book make clear, there are a staggering number of software programs, applications, and tools at their disposal. These technologies can be used in a variety of ways, for a wide range of purposes, and can have a myriad of intended and unintended consequences. The problem is that keeping up with technological change can be a job in itself. The value of this book lies in its comprehensive approach to identifying key issues related to social media and student affairs, providing concrete examples wherein social media has been used for specific purposes, and initiating conversations about how to incorporate these technologies into established communication routines.

INTRODUCTION

OUTLINE OF THE BOOK

Each subsequent chapter addresses an important facet of student affairs, roughly tracking the life cycle of individuals as they progress from being a prospective student, to an enrolled student, to a graduate of the institution. Chapter 1 explores the use of social media in admissions and enrollment. Chapter 2 examines social media use in academic services, including advising and mentoring. Chapter 3 investigates social media's complex relationship with student health and well-being. Chapter 4 considers how social media affects institutions' ability to provide a safe and vibrant campus. Chapter 5 reviews how career services and alumni services are using social media to assist them in the myriad services they provide to current and former students. The final chapter of the book places these discussions into a larger context that involves a mixture of organizational policy, resources, and communication strategies.

The chapters begin by reviewing the roles of these respective units and discussing how they performed their duties in the past. They then address how student affairs professionals in these units have incorporated social media into their routines, evidenced by specific examples from a wide variety of institutions. The challenges associated with social media use, as well as strategies for overcoming them, are addressed in these discussions. Each chapter closes with a list of questions designed to stimulate discussions about how the concepts and examples found in the chapter might translate to one's own institution. For instance, the questions at the end of this chapter are designed to get student affairs professionals thinking broadly about how their office and their colleagues currently interact with social media. This organizational structure is intended to help student affairs professionals think about the use of social media in a thoughtful, strategic way. Individuals can read the book from start to finish or simply focus on the chapter(s) specifically related to their position.

DISCUSSION QUESTIONS

- Are your student affairs colleagues better characterized as technophiles, technophobes, or somewhere in between?

- Do they have a basic understanding of the key characteristics associated with social media technologies?
- What social media platforms are they comfortable using? How much training would be required to make them proficient using other platforms?
- What resources are available? How are those resources being used to pursue strategic goals? What goals are being pursued? How do you measure whether or not goals are being met?
- What does the unit's social media presence look like? What platforms are being used? How often is material posted to these accounts? Who is responsible for posting that material?

NOTES

1. See, e.g., Tess 2013; Allen 2012; Wood et al. 2011.
2. Steinfield et al. 2008; Madge et al. 2009.
3. Waite and Wheeler 2016.
4. See Baier and Strong 1994; Kruger 2005; Cabellon and Junco 2015.
5. Long 2012.
6. Detailed treatments of the student affairs field include Zhang 2011; McClellen and Stringer 2016.
7. Hirt 2006.
8. Long 2012.
9. ACPA 1937.
10. ACPA 1949.
11. Long 2012; Hirt 2006.
12. Long 2012.
13. Hirt 2006.
14. Baier 1994.
15. Mills 1990, 138.
16. Miller 1994.
17. Strong 1994.
18. Elling and Brown 2001.
19. Burnett 2002.
20. College Student Educators International 2015.
21. Burnett 2002, 92.

1

SOCIAL MEDIA STRATEGIES FOR RECRUITMENT, ADMISSIONS, AND ENROLLMENT

The basic business model of higher education is relatively easy to understand. Students want to attend universities that can help them achieve their goals. Universities want to attract students who are likely to succeed and must seal the deal by encouraging accepted applicants to enroll. Of course, this simple relationship between recruitment, admissions, and enrollment belies a complex set of goals and challenges. This chapter examines how universities approach recruitment, admissions, and enrollment routines, with an emphasis on the ways that student affairs professionals are leveraging new media technologies to accomplish their tasks.

Understanding the journey students take to reach their decisions regarding higher education is critical to crafting successful recruitment strategies. Each year, students progress through a cycle that has three broad stages, resulting in a recruitment funnel (see figure 1.1). In the first stage, the institution builds awareness and generates a pool of applicants. In the second stage, the institution selects its class by employing a variety of admissions procedures and protocols. And in the third stage, the institution yields its class by securing firm acceptances and enrolling students in classes. Online technologies have become useful tools for addressing the unique challenges posed at each stage.

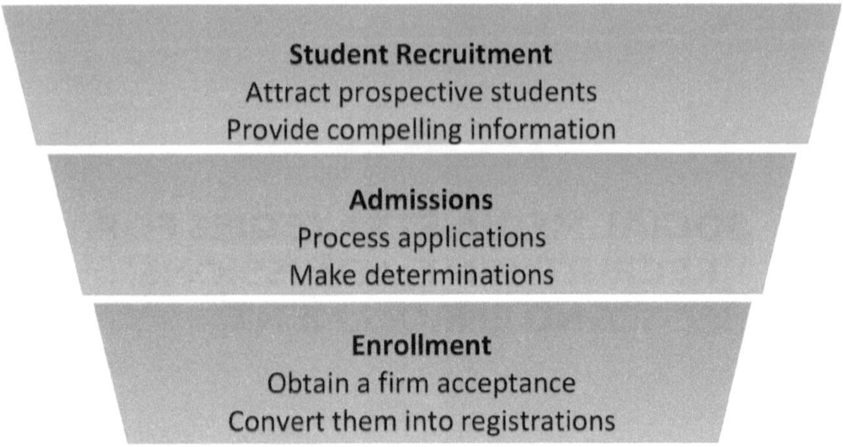

Student Recruitment
Attract prospective students
Provide compelling information

Admissions
Process applications
Make determinations

Enrollment
Obtain a firm acceptance
Convert them into registrations

Figure 1.1. Enrollment funnel

STUDENT RECRUITMENT

The first stage is shaped by the university's strategic plan, which lays out a path for achieving sustainable growth among other things. Broadly speaking, these plans seek to reduce the institution's reliance on a small number of markets and increase its reputation. The nuances of the plan reflect the institution's unique values, resources, and market niche. When done correctly, these plans establish recruitment goals and provide some guidance on how faculty, staff, and administrators should pursue them. A university's strategic plan should identify which student populations to target for recruitment and what institutional characteristics should be highlighted in order to attract their attention.

Recruitment Challenges

The context for recruitment plans has changed significantly over the last decade. Today, the competition for students has reached a fevered pitch. There are a variety of reasons for this, including economic uncertainty, increased competition, changing demographic trends, and changing student expectations.

While many families' ability to pay for college in recent years has diminished, the cost of college tuition and student fees has steadily risen (even after accounting for other variables like financial aid). More families are reevaluating what they are willing to pay and focusing more attention on the return on investment of majoring in certain fields. They are considering factors such as cost, reputation, and evidence of successful results (e.g., graduation rates and alumni employment statistics) to justify their investment.[1]

At the same time that families have become more discerning, traditional academic institutions have faced increasing competition from for-profit schools, online universities, and vocational programs. More students are attending multiple institutions in pursuit of a degree, often completing courses from the core curriculum at less expensive two-year public institutions before transferring to four-year institutions to complete their degree. There are also concerns that the number of programs available to international students in the United States, Canada, Britain, Australia, and other English-speaking countries will soon outstrip the number of these students in the market.[2]

Meanwhile, the number of high school graduates is shrinking due to a dip in the birth rate, particularly in the Midwest and Northeast. In recent years the percentage increase in the number of students ages twenty-five and over has been larger than the percentage increase in the number of younger students.[3] One might expect recruitment challenges will become even more challenging as older individuals get drawn back into an improving economy.

Colleges and universities are also grappling with changing expectations. In addition to evaluating institutions' resources and credentials, prospective students now attempt to ascertain how they would fit in at the institution. Incoming classes of students are becoming more ethnically and religiously diverse, making it imperative for institutions to convey indicators of acceptance and inclusivity. These campus life indicators can be more important for many students than those associated with prestige or outcomes. And finally, students and their families expect information about all these facets of the institution to be available at their fingertips on devices that can fit in their pockets.[4]

Recruitment Marketing

The goal is always the same: recruit applicants. To achieve this goal, universities must figure out how to use the appropriate tools (e.g., paid advertisements, websites, emails, and social media) to provide the right audiences (e.g., parents and students) with the right information (e.g., credentials, rankings, resources, opportunities, curricula, career options, and campus life indicators) at the right time in the recruitment cycle (e.g., initial search, psychosocial moratorium, and action) to encourage a specific action (e.g., request additional information, apply for financial aid, schedule a campus tour, or apply for admission).

To deal with this complexity, universities are bringing together marketing and communications professionals who understand big data; student affairs professionals who understand recruitment and enrollment; and the faculty, staff, and administrators responsible for implementing social media initiatives. They are collectively crafting and implementing strategies that must be routinely fine-tuned as the effectiveness of various marketing tactics, popularity of individual platforms, and rules of engagement between brands and students change.

Locating Target Audiences

When high school students register to take the Pre-Scholastic Aptitude Test (PSAT), the Scholastic Aptitude Test (SAT), or the American College Testing (ACT), they are asked a series of questions about their grades, family income, interests, intended major, and the types of colleges that might interest them. Their answers to these questions yield dozens of data points that are sold with the student's name and contact information to colleges and scholarship services. Universities have historically purchased as many names as they can afford and based their projections of class size on this number.

Enrollment growth strategies have been largely based on taking the demographics of the previous year's freshman class and simply purchasing more names that matched those characteristics. At one point, Saint Louis University was purchasing upward of 250,000 names annually.[5] In 2010 alone, the College Board sold eighty million names to approximately 1,200 colleges and universities[6] at a cost of thirty-two cents per name (a cost that had risen to forty-two cents per name by 2017).[7]

Taking a cue from marketing practices in the private sector, colleges and universities are scaling back their name purchases from testing companies and focusing more of their resources on companies that use big data and social media to better pinpoint prospects, often as early as their sophomore year in high school. This shift has had a profound impact on the recruitment timeline. Given that testing companies release their lists of student names once a year, recruitment strategies were anchored around this date. The goal for student affairs professionals was to obtain the names on the day they were released and get recruitment materials mailed immediately in an effort to reach students before they were flooded with similar materials from other institutions. Recruitment marketing now persists year-round.

Rather than purchasing advertising space on a specific website, and then hoping the institution's target audience visits that site, marketers can now target their advertisements to individuals who fit the characteristics of a certain demographic on whatever sites they visit. These characteristics can include any number of demographics (e.g., age, gender, ethnicity) as well as psychographics, which measure customers' attitudes and interests.[8] Not only does this enable universities to aim their advertising at a target-rich environment, but it can also be a tremendous asset for institutions seeking to increase the number of applications submitted by historically underrepresented groups, foreign students, or out-of-state students.

Marketers can also tweak their advertisements to see what works best for each audience. For instance, the chief marketing officer at Cleveland State University found that online advertisements informing students they could save $5,000 in tuition and room and board by participating in a freshman scholars program outperformed a similar advertisement that said they could save 30 percent.[9]

Online advertising also allows marketers to track the behavior of those who click on these advertisements. If an individual clicks on a university's advertisement on Spotify and begins filling out an online application but fails to finish it, the institution can later target that individual with another advertisement on Spotify (or even another social network) reminding him or her to complete the application process.

Recruitment Stages and Social Media Strategies

Locating students is only half the battle. Institutions must then provide them with relevant information in order to convince them to apply. Making matters more difficult, the relevance of certain types of information changes over time. While recruitment efforts never stop, they can be roughly divided into three phases that correspond to the needs and behaviors of students and their parents: an initial search phase, a psychosocial moratorium phase, and an action phase. Social media is becoming a vital part of university strategies in all three phases.

Initial Search Phase

During the initial search phase, prospective students and their parents seek answers to basic questions regarding the institution's credentials, rankings, accreditations, applicant data, costs, admissions requirements, placement of graduates, and contact information. Universities have traditionally communicated these types of information by dispatching recruitment officers to high schools and disseminating a plethora of printed materials to prospective students and their families. While universities still use these traditional means of communication, studies suggest that most students now prefer to receive information through electronic sources such as websites and social media channels.[10] Today, institutions use a variety of online tools to supplement their ultimate sales and marketing device: the campus tour.

University websites have proven to be an essential tool for communicating these types of factual information about the institution. These websites are considered the "ultimate brand statement" of an institution.[11] Universities focus a significant amount of resources on pay-per-click advertising, search engine optimization, and mobile marketing to drive traffic to their websites.

In order to capture and retain the interest of prospective students, it is important for university websites to be informative, visually appealing, and easy to use. Great care is taken to ensure that these websites are consistently designed and easily navigable. University websites are increasingly being optimized for smartphones and tablets to aid with visual design and usability. This reflects an emerging mobile-first mindset.

They also feature well-placed navigation bars, search tools, and calls to action (e.g., "Apply Now" buttons). Elements such as videos, slideshows, and other multimedia content can help appeal to distinct target markets and provide a conduit to content they will find valuable. As one might imagine, it can be a challenge for universities to create a website that appeals to a diverse range of visitors (e.g., prospective students, current students, and alumni) while staying intuitive and uncluttered.

Given that students flock to social media platforms en masse and use them to conduct extensive research on colleges and universities, institutions are increasingly incorporating these technologies into their strategies to reach students during their initial search phase. Faculty and staff are often eager to utilize them as well since these platforms allow for greater control over communications. And marketing and communications experts recognize their successful use in the business sector and hope to replicate that success on campus. Given that the demonstrable outcomes of social media marketing include improved communications, customer engagement, and brand loyalty, it is reasonable to expect these efforts to help bolster universities' recruitment and enrollment efforts.

The ability for anyone to create a social media profile on behalf of an institution or unit has its drawbacks, including questions of authenticity and consistency. In the past, concerns regarding credibility and lack of engagement by institutions hampered these types of efforts on social media.[12] These issues were particularly problematic during social media's infancy, when higher-education professionals were quick to experiment with emerging platforms—often with little to no oversight or coordination—and just as quick to abandon them.

As social media became more ubiquitous, faculty, staff, and administrators became more committed to engaging various stakeholders using these online platforms. Universities began developing policies regarding the creation of institutional accounts on social media as well as aggregating and auditing such accounts. As institutional accounts became more established, consistent, and interactive, they also became more trusted.

Nearly three-fourths of students in a recent study reported using social media for gathering information about colleges and universities to which they are applying.[13] These online platforms are particularly important sources of information for individuals who do not have the financial resources to make campus visits, those who lack access to adequate mentoring and counseling, and those who may be unable to rely on their family for mentoring (e.g., first-generation college students). While social media may be *supplementing* some students' initial search activities, they may be wholly *supplanting* some of those activities for other students.

The key to converting prospects into applicants is to identify and capitalize on engagement opportunities as they emerge. Universities are finding it imperative to engage in the act of monitoring social media to ascertain what people are saying about and to the institution. This practice, called *social listening*, is particularly important during the initial search phase, when prospective students and their parents are actively seeking answers to questions and weighing their options.

In addition to social listening, many universities are using social media to actively solicit questions from prospective students. Pennsylvania State University encouraged students and their families to participate in a series of hour-long "chat sessions" on Twitter by tweeting their questions about the application process to @PSUWorldCampus using the hashtag #ChatPSUWC.[14] Admissions counselors were prepared to immediately tweet their responses to these inquiries during these sessions.

Other schools, such as Dartmouth College, have hosted similar live chat sessions between admissions officers and prospective students on Facebook.[15]

Popular photography-centered social networks like Snapchat and Instagram have also proven useful for reaching students during their initial search phase. A handful of colleges and universities have used Snapchat's geofilters—the special overlays (e.g., a university logo) that can only be accessed by users when they are in certain locations—to increase brand awareness. The presence of the geofilter signals to users that they are currently in a designated area (e.g., on campus). Applying the filter to your photo provides a fun way to show friends and followers you have visited the location. Not only are these geofilters fun for prospective students to use while visiting campus, but they can also get

RECRUITMENT, ADMISSIONS, AND ENROLLMENT

people's attention as they pass through an area. This can be an important asset for universities that reside in rural areas that may be overlooked by interstate travelers as well as those in dense urban areas where campus boundaries may be difficult to ascertain.

Some institutions have worked to link their online and offline recruitment efforts. For instance, when *Popular Science* named a resource on Texas Tech's campus one of the country's "Most Awesome College Labs," the university decided to feature that honor in its annual recruiting mailer. During the photo shoot for the mailer, when photographers and producers were bustling around setting up lighting and camera equipment, the university provided behind-the-scenes footage of the action on Twitter. The goal was to make students feel like they were part of an event rather than just the recipient of a piece of mail.[16]

Psychosocial Moratorium Phase

The initial search phase concludes once students and their families change their focus from information about academic quality and procedures to indicators of institutional fit. They express more interest in learning about residence halls, campus events, clubs and organizations, dining options, athletic programs, and other signals of what life is like at the institution. These types of information better enable prospects to imagine how they would fare as a student at that institution. The process of comparing and contrasting these imagined selves in search of an identity-crisis resolution is called psychosocial moratorium.[17]

The transition from the initial search phase to the psychosocial moratorium phase often occurs as a result of the campus tour. Simply put, it is much easier to imagine oneself as a student at the institution when one walks across its campus. Study after study has demonstrated that a campus visit is the single most influential determinant for students when making their decision about which college to attend.[18] Recognizing the pivotal nature of campus visits, student affairs and marketing professionals have found ways to use online technologies to make the most of the "Golden Mile."

———∽∽∽———

Schools now routinely ask visitors to share their photographs of campus on social media using designated hashtags. Some even create marketing gimmicks to entice individuals into doing so. For example, marketing professionals at the University of Wisconsin–Madison cut the center out of a large corrugated plastic sign to create a red frame, upon which they printed #FutureBadgers on one side (for use with larger groups) and #FutureBadger on the other (for single student pictures).[19] Campus visitors were given the opportunity to get their picture taken while holding the frame and were encouraged to share the picture on social media. This gave prospective students an opportunity to share the excitement of their campus tour experience with their peers on social media.

———∽∽∽———

The "high-touch" experience of a campus tour can be supplemented with "high-tech" digital storytelling. Universities are increasingly using platforms such as Facebook, Twitter, YouTube, Instagram, and Snapchat to provide students with opportunities to learn more about campus life. In fact, these tools can usher students into the psychosocial moratorium phase long before they step foot on campus.

One of the most successful tactics universities use is to have *current* students create social media posts that communicate the messages universities wish to communicate to prospective students. This allows prospective students to see and hear about the campus from an authentic perspective. Universities have implemented this tactic in a variety of ways.

One means of doing so simply involves giving a student the "keys to the account" for a day. When done correctly, these day-in-the-life-of stories reflect the personality of the individual entrusted with making the posts and showcase the kinds of campus resources and activities that prospective students will find appealing. This storytelling mechanism has become a popular marketing tactic both inside and outside of higher education.

RECRUITMENT, ADMISSIONS, AND ENROLLMENT

Mimicking the show *Cribs* on Music Television (more commonly known as MTV), which featured tours of mansions owned by celebrities, the University of Southern California created a YouTube playlist called USC Cribs. The videos in the playlist showed prospective students the living conditions on campus by taking them on tours of students' rooms in the university's various residence halls.[20]

Rather than seeing a professionally produced segment, viewers were treated to an unrefined look into the lives of real students. While listening to the room's occupants discuss the unique characteristics of each residence hall and the tactics for overcoming the challenges of living with roommates, viewers caught glimpses of unmade beds and dishes left unwashed because there were more exciting things to do. It is easy to see how these videos can spark the imagination of prospective students.

Georgetown University took this concept a step further by selecting a cast of more than a dozen students and having them film their experiences on and off campus throughout the year. The students created videos of them moving into their residence halls, attending tailgate parties, engaging in classroom and laboratory activities, participating in intermural sports, studying for midterm exams, and a host of other experiences.[21] The videos were featured on Georgetown's Facebook, Twitter, Instagram, and SnapChat accounts with the hashtag #GeorgetownStories.

During the first year of this initiative, the number of Instagram users that interacted with the university's account increased by 2,007 percent, while the number of engaged users on Facebook increased by 348 percent.[22] The project was so successful that the university replicated it in successive years, each time following a different cast of students.

Action Phase

At long last, prospective students apply to their chosen colleges and universities. Institutions have taken great strides to ensure prospective students have no problem finding their way to the university's online application portal once they are ready to initiate action. It is standard practice for university websites to prominently feature "Apply Now" buttons. Printed recruitment materials typically contain short, unambiguous Internet addresses (e.g., www.apply.msstate.edu) and may also employ other tactics to guide people to the online application portal, such as Quick Response (QR) codes that enable smartphone applications to access information (e.g., a link to an online application) by taking a picture of black-and-white pixelated labels containing the code. Social media posts often contain a link to the online application as well.

The fact that colleges and universities have worked to make their application systems easier to locate and use does not address the fact that prospective students are still required to fill out a unique application—with a unique set of requirements—for each institution. While initiatives aimed at standardizing application processes, such as the Common Application (which has 700 member colleges) and the Coalition for Access, Affordability, and Success (140 member institutions), have helped mitigate this issue, most students and their families must still contend with a separate set of procedures to apply for some form of financial aid. Given the tedious and confusing nature of these procedures, many students who begin the application process never finish it.

Universities have employed a variety of measures to combat this problem, including sending emails with step-by-step instructions, hosting instructional webinars, and making follow-up phone calls. These approaches are now being supplemented with social media initiatives that help students and their families navigate these complicated and confusing application procedures. Student affairs professionals now use sites like Facebook, Twitter, YouTube, Instagram, and Snapchat to clarify terms (e.g., whether a student is classified as a "dependent" or not) and explain what documents need to be gathered to complete the application process (e.g., financial aid and tax forms). Social media can also be invaluable for providing applicants with timely tips, deadline reminders, and words of encouragement.

Videos can be particularly useful for communicating the byzantine information that students and their families might otherwise have trouble understanding. A case in point, Colorado State University's YouTube channel featured a playlist titled "Office of Admissions," where student affairs professionals provided detailed information about the application process in videos with titles such as "How to Apply and Pay for College," "Coming to CSU as a Transfer Student," and "What You Need to Know as an International Student."[23] The videos featured admissions counselors, financial aid officers, international programs staff, student ambassadors, and others explaining the nuanced steps of various application processes.

Colleges and universities want to usher students from initial search to action as quickly as possible. Early action applications offer a means of doing so. *Early action* refers to an option where students submit an application by a specific deadline in return for a decision well in advance of the institution's regular response date. More than a third of four-year colleges and universities in the United States offer an early action application option. The lower an institution's yield rate (discussed in the Enrollment Challenges and Solutions section of this chapter), the more likely it is to employ such an option.[24]

ADMISSIONS

Once an institution has generated a pool of applicants, it must select its class. To accomplish this, college admissions officers are tasked with reviewing applications and determining which students receive an offer to attend the institution. Changing expectations and technological advancements have garnered these review processes a significant amount of attention in recent years.

Colleges want to attract students who will be successful. It does neither the student nor the college any good to admit a student who is likely to fail. The question then becomes, what metrics are the best predictors of student success in college?

Colleges have traditionally considered grade point averages and standardized test scores to be the primary indicators of college readiness. However, as the utility of these measures has come into question, admissions offices have turned to other, more subjective, means of assessing applicants. It is not uncommon now for universities to require applicants to submit a cover letter, writing sample, or personal statement. Some universities even consider checking the social media accounts of their applicants for egregious behavior that, if discovered at a later time, might bring the college or university into disrepute. This latter tactic is not without controversy.

Problems Associated with Traditional Admissions Criteria

Some have argued that grade point averages are becoming less helpful for differentiating between applicants as a result of grade inflation. A recent study found that between 1998 and 2016, the average high school grade point average went from 3.27 to 3.38 (on a four-point scale). These gains were most pronounced at rural high schools and those that consisted of mostly white students and students who were wealthier than average.[25] This leaves minority students and those in less affluent districts at a disadvantage in the college admissions process.

One might wonder if grade inflation is the result of students becoming better educated or smarter. The authors of the study suggest this is not the case, noting that as grade point averages increased, students' SAT scores fell. From 1998 to 2018, SAT averages (math and verbal; 1,600-point scale) fell from 1,026 to 1,002.[26] The study's authors point to this discrepancy as evidence that colleges and universities need standardized tests like the SAT to accurately judge students' abilities.

Others suggest an alternative explanation for the discrepancy, noting that the population of students taking the SAT changed significantly during this time period. Some states, such as Illinois, began requiring all high school students to take the SAT. As more students took the exam, average scores dropped. Further complicating matters is the fact that the SAT was redesigned during this time period, making comparisons between cohorts more difficult.

Some have even questioned the motivations of the aforementioned study's authors, one of whom (Michael Hurwitz) worked for the College Board. One critic noted that it was in the College Board's financial interest to erode trust in high school grade point averages, likening the study to "the tobacco institute doing research on healthy lifestyles."[27] Even absent such charges, there may be other reasons to question the use of standardized tests in college admissions.

Critics have pointed out the fact that the SAT emphasizes speed—quick recall and time management—rather than subject knowledge. The SAT is also norm-referenced rather than criterion-referenced.[28] In other words, the exam is designed to rank students by comparing them to other test takers (and thus producing a bell curve distribution among examinees) rather than measure their performance against fixed academic standards (which would make it possible for a larger proportion of examinees to score well). Given that answering a few more questions correctly can substantially raise students' scores (and thus their ranking), students who cannot afford test-prep materials that help them develop time-management skills (e.g., strategies and practice tests) are at a clear disadvantage.

Students who are not comfortable taking standardized tests may be deterred from applying to colleges that require them. Research has shown that underrepresented groups are more likely than others to be deterred by such requirements.[29] Thus, in addition to questions regarding the extent to which standardized test scores are indicative of students' potential in college, some institutions worry that requiring such tests may reduce the size and diversity of their applicant pools.

An entire industry exists to help increase the likelihood of acceptance for those who can afford such services. In addition to SAT preparation materials and courses, some companies offer assistance crafting cover letters, writing samples, and other application materials. Other services include conducting mock interviews and etiquette training.

Many companies now offer services that help students craft digital narratives that admissions officers will find attractive. Their advice to students includes things like creating a personal website, recording videos of themselves using their talents and strengths to benefit others, and storing and organizing fine arts projects in online portfolios. Students are also increasingly receiving advice about the content they post to their social media profiles.

Reviewing Students' Online Behavior in the Admissions Process

The debate surrounding whether or not universities should review, or monitor, students' online behavior has intensified in recent years. Some have argued that universities have a responsibility to ensure the safety of their campus and students and thus bear a responsibility to identify security threats regardless of where they emerge. This argument has gained traction as cyber-bullying has become more salient in the field of education. Others have argued that the First Amendment trumps professional norms and that students' constitutional rights are often violated when schools punish them for content posted on their social media profiles.

The right of schools to review students' speech has been hotly contested for decades. In *Tinker v. Des Moines Community School District* (1969), the Supreme Court affirmed that students' free speech rights are not suspended when they step foot on campus but noted that such rights are not absolute. Ruling that school officials cannot regulate speech merely to avoid discomfort or unpleasantness (e.g., forbidding students from wearing black armbands in protest of military conflicts in Vietnam), the court recognized the right of schools to extend academic disciplinary measures to speech that could reasonably lead "school officials to forecast substantial disruption of or material interference with school activities."[30]

The courts have had to decide when circumstances warrant an application of the *Tinker* standard. In *Bethel School District v. Fraser* (1986), the Supreme Court held that the constitutional rights of students at public school are not automatically coextensive with the rights of adults, ruling that schools could discipline students for using vulgar and offensive language in the school setting in order to maintain discipline.[31]

In *Hazelwood School District v. Kuhlmeier* (1988), the Supreme Court noted that the rights of students are applied "in light of the special characteristics of the school environment," ruling that schools could regulate student speech where it might reasonably be perceived to "bear the imprimatur of the school" (e.g., student-authored articles in the school newspaper).[32] Furthermore, the courts have applied the *Tinker* standard regardless of where the speech originated or how it reached campus. For instance, in *Morse v. Frederick* (2007), the Supreme Court ruled that school administrators could discipline students for certain types of speech (e.g., holding a banner bearing the words "Bong Hits 4 Jesus") at school-supervised events taking place off campus.

These Supreme Court decisions set the stage for cases involving students' speech on social media. The most notable of these is *Keefe v. Adams* (2016), a case that involved a student who was expelled from the nursing program at Central Lakes College after Facebook posts that he made on his public personal account—including one describing a fellow classmate as a "stupid bitch"—were brought to administrators' attention. The expelled student, Craig Keefe, filed a lawsuit in a U.S. District Court arguing that the school administrators had violated his First Amendment rights. He contended that the college had violated his due process rights by characterizing his expulsion as an "academic" rather than a "disciplinary" decision. This distinction is important given that colleges have significant leeway in arranging their academic misconduct proceedings, whereas their disciplinary proceedings must offer basic due process protections (e.g., adequate notice and right to appeal). When the district court dismissed Keefe's case against the university, he appealed to the Eighth Circuit Court of Appeals.

In a split 2–1 decision, the appeals court also ruled against Keefe, arguing that college administrators and educators have "the discretion to require compliance with recognized standards of the profession, both on and off campus," so long as their actions are "reasonably related to legitimate pedagogical concerns."[33] The court refused to classify the proceeding as "academic" or "disciplinary" since it held that the college had not violated Keefe's due process rights regardless of the characterization. The ruling shocked many legal observers, some of whom worried that the Eighth Circuit had opened the door for colleges and universities to punish students for exercising their First Amendment rights.

Keefe appealed his case to the Supreme Court, arguing that the Eighth Circuit ruling unjustly allowed public colleges and universities to discipline students for speech that has no relation to the professional context in a particular field. The Student Press Law Center joined four other free-expression advocacy groups in filing an amicus brief in support of Keefe. They argued that colleges cannot punish off-campus speech merely because they (or some other private organization) regard it as "unprofessional" and that off-campus speech is entitled to greater protection than that which occurs inside the classroom during school.[34]

The Supreme Court declined to hear Keefe's case. As a result, colleges and universities are seemingly well within their right to take action against students for a potentially wide range of speech that is inconsistent with their (subjective) understanding of professionalism, including that which takes place online. There appears to be nothing stopping these institutions from applying these standards to *prospective* students either.

Even if admissions officers do not make a habit of reviewing applicants' social media profiles, they can find themselves in the position of having to define what constitutes unacceptable behavior and decide what to do when confronted with evidence that applicants have exhibited such behavior online.

In the winter of 2016, a handful of students admitted to Harvard College created a messaging group to share funny memes about popular culture. They used the university's official Harvard College Class of 2021 Facebook page to find and invite other admitted students to join the chat. The posts were lighthearted and inoffensive, prompting some members of the (unofficial) group to create an R-rated version of the meme chat.

The university's administrators were soon confronted with evidence that some recently admitted students were sharing racist and sexually explicit images in a private Facebook group chat titled Harvard Memes for Horny Bourgeois Teens. The images included memes mocking sexual assault, victims of pedophilia, and victims of the Holocaust. The incident ended with Harvard rescinding the offers of at least ten students who had participated in the chat.[35]

Another incident occurred in 2017, when an employee of a private school noticed a social media post created by one of the school's students indicating that she was about to enroll in the University of Rochester. Finding it odd that the student had not indicated she was applying to Rochester, nor asked for her transcripts to be sent to the university, the employee notified university officials that something suspicious was afoot. It turned out that the student deliberately misled the university to believe that she was home-schooled, presumably with higher credentials than she actually earned at the private school. The student was immediately removed from campus and kicked out of the university.[36]

While instances like these are headline grabbing, it is difficult to know the true extent to which college admissions officers review applicants' social media profiles. Research on the subject is relatively sparse. Those who believe the practice is common often point to a 2017 survey conducted by Kaplan Test Prep in which more than a third of college admissions officers admitted to checking applicants' social media profiles, and 42 percent of those who did so reported that what they found had a negative impact on their review of the applicant.[37]

Others suggest that a survey conducted that same year by Inside Higher Ed and Gallup is more reliable. This survey of college and university admissions directors found that only 2 percent of public institutions, and 13 percent of private institutions, have admissions officers routinely check applicants' social media accounts. Asked if colleges *should* check applicants' accounts, only 15 percent of respondents from public institutions, and 14 percent of those at private institutions, said "yes."[38]

Skeptics often point out the time and effort it would take to conduct systematic reviews of applicants' various social media accounts, arguing that colleges and universities do not have the resources to do so even if they wanted to. Some have even suggested that companies specializing in helping students with the application process are deliberately inflating perceptions of the practice in order to sell costly audits of their customers' social media accounts. Time will tell if these types of audits are warranted.

ENROLLMENT

In the final stage of the enrollment funnel, institutions must obtain a firm acceptance from admitted students and convert these acceptances into registrations. Achieving this goal has become increasingly difficult over time. The number of admitted students who actually enroll in classes—known as the yield rate—has been in freefall for years at all but the most elite universities.[39] In 2016, the average yield rate among universities in the United States was 32 percent. That rate was only 27 percent among smaller liberal arts colleges.[40]

Strategies to combat this problem can leave institutions chasing their own tail, so to speak. If the goal is to reach a certain class size, one means of accounting for falling yield rates is to simply increase the number of applicants who are admitted. However, institutions have an interest in keeping this ratio as low as possible given that students and their parents often view the admit rate (i.e., the percentage of applicants admitted) as a proxy for quality. Colleges can reduce admit rates by working to increase the number of applications but often do so by increasing the number of "soft" applicants who have a lower propensity to enroll. Thus, as an institution's admit rate falls, so too does its yield rate. This strategy is an expensive means of reaching target class sizes given the costs associated with managing and reviewing applications.

This has driven colleges and universities to seek out alternative strategies for reaching target class sizes that do not rely on increasing the number of applications they receive. Many institutions are rethinking the ways they communicate with admitted students to help them overcome the various challenges that prevent them from enrolling. Not surprisingly, student affairs professionals have turned to social media to support these efforts.

Enrollment Challenges and Solutions

There are a number of reasons that admitted students may fail to enroll in classes at an institution. Students may decide to attend another college to which they have also been accepted. Or they may get flummoxed by the financial aid process and decide that college is unaffordable. Others may succumb to anxiousness about being away from their parents or leaving the comfort of their hometown. And some may simply not understand various registration, housing, and orientation processes. Universities have found that personal outreach efforts can go a long way to addressing these challenges, making social media a valuable tool at this stage.

Most students apply to more than one college or university. As a result, many students receive several (competing) offers of acceptance. Some students may even confirm their acceptance to multiple institutions simultaneously, perhaps even putting down several deposits, until they make up their minds. This creates an enormous challenge for student affairs professionals who are tasked with predicting class sizes and meeting these expectations.

RECRUITMENT, ADMISSIONS, AND ENROLLMENT

To mitigate this problem, some institutions offer an early decision application option. *Early decision* refers to an option where students commit to enrolling if admitted by the institution. Students pursue this option in hopes that their commitment will increase their chances of being accepted. Given the binding nature of early decision application options, they typically result in a much higher yield rate than their nonbinding counterparts (87 percent compared to 26 percent). Research suggests that elite private colleges are more likely than public institutions to offer early decision options (29 percent compared to 7 percent). It is worth noting here that early action application options, discussed previously in this chapter, do not appear to increase yield rates.[41]

There are other strategies for increasing yield rates that do not rely on special application procedures. One such strategy is to make admitted individuals *feel* like a student in hopes that they will actually commit to *being* one. Traditional tactics include sending students university-branded bric-a-brac such as pens, pendants, coffee mugs, and USB flash drives.

More recently, student affairs professionals have begun inviting admitted students to university-related Facebook pages and groups (e.g., University of Iowa Class of 2021). These pages and groups, which are discussed at length in the next chapter, connect admitted students with those who have already enrolled. By enabling student affairs professionals to routinely communicate information to admitted students and fostering a sense of belonging, these pages have the potential to alleviate the anxiety of those who may be reluctant to leave home for college.

There are other ways to leverage social media to demonstrate to nervous students that they are not going to experience the transition to college alone. For example, Misericordia University in Pennsylvania ran a two-week contest during the summer where incoming freshmen were offered university bookstore gift certificates for replacing their Facebook profile picture with the university logo.[42] Not only was the contest fun for those who participated, but it also had the effect of showing others who were considering attending the institution that they would not be among total strangers when they arrived.

Other institutions have hosted similar initiatives wherein admitted students are asked to post a picture of themselves holding their acceptance letter to their social media channels using a specific hashtag. Many universities send acceptance packets in packaging that is tailor-made for sharing the experience on social media. Case in point: in 2016, acceptance letters from Indiana University came in an envelope bearing the hashtag #IUsaidYes.[43]

Another solution is to host online events, such as chat sessions, that connect admitted students with current students. For instance, Georgetown University hosted a series of online chat sessions for admitted students where questions related to student life, academic requirements, transfer credits, and other issues of interest to students and their parents could be addressed.[44] These types of peer-to-peer initiatives can alleviate the concerns of admitted students and convince them to enroll.

Universities can also urge admitted students to further explore the curricular and extracurricular opportunities available on campus in an effort to solicit and maintain their commitment during this stage. Many universities maintain a social media directory of some kind, which can help facilitate this kind of independent online exploration. This highlights the importance of promoting a strong Internet technology culture on campus.[45] Content posted on these networks can simultaneously communicate different messages to distinct audiences, thereby achieving wildly different goals.

While passively introducing admitted students to the range of clubs and organizations on campus can help maintain their interest, it can also be advantageous to challenge students to actively engage and share content with their peers. For example, Westminster College hosted a con-

RECRUITMENT, ADMISSIONS, AND ENROLLMENT

test called Trippin' with Griffin, wherein the school sent a small paper cutout of the school's mascot to admitted students and invited them to post a creative picture of it on the school's Facebook page for a chance to win a digital video camera.[46] Fun contests like these can help keep students excited and engaged with the institution.

Universities can also entice individuals to enroll by piquing their interest in specific courses and programs. Taking inspiration from the dating application Tinder, wherein users are shown pictures of other users who are located nearby and given the option of swiping left (to signal disinterest) or right (to signal interest) by touching the screen, the University of Salford created a smartphone application called Match Made in Salford. The application presented users with potential courses based on the student's career interests. Students could swipe left to dismiss the suggestion or swipe right to signal their interest in the course. Once the user indicated he or she was done swiping, the application provided the student with a personalized list of possible courses, including detailed information about the program, fees, and career options.[47]

CONCLUSION

The importance of recruitment, admissions, and enrollment is reflected in the allocation of resources. One of the noticeable trends in higher education is the increasing amount of time and money universities are investing in branding and marketing efforts. Colleges and universities are hiring marketing professionals from the corporate world and putting technology at the center of their branding and marketing approaches by focusing on responsive website design, search engine optimization, mobile development, and strategic social media.[48] The following questions speak to these choices and strategies being developed by colleges and universities across the country.

DISCUSSION QUESTIONS

- How are big data analytics being used to target prospective students? Are these individuals receiving the right messages at the right times on the right platforms?
- Can prospective students take a virtual tour of campus? What is featured in the virtual tour? What is missing?
- Do social media posts provide individuals with relevant information and enable them to take action by linking them to appropriate websites and the institution's application portal?
- Do admissions officials review prospective students' social media sites? Are there any policies regarding this activity?

NOTES

1. Hanover Research 2014.
2. Ibid.
3. National Center for Education Statistics 2012.
4. Rogers 2015.
5. Selingo 2017a.
6. Hoover 2010.
7. Selingo 2017b.
8. Samuel 2016.
9. Farkas 2014.
10. Noel-Levitz 2017.
11. Higher Education Marketing 2013.
12. Constantinides and Stagno 2011.
13. Rogers 2014.
14. Pennsylvania State University 2015.
15. Dartmouth College 2014.
16. Lytle 2011.
17. Erikson 1968.
18. Okerson 2016.
19. Magellan Promotions n.d.
20. Daily Trojan 2015.
21. *Georgetown Stories* n.d.
22. Williams 2017.
23. Colorado State University 2019.
24. National Association for College Admission Counseling 2015.

25. Hurwitz and Lee 2018.
26. Ibid.
27. Curmudgucation 2017.
28. Atkinson and Geiser 2015.
29. Steele 1997.
30. *Tinker v. Des Moines Indep. Cmty. School Dist.* 1969, at 514.
31. *Bethel School District v. Fraser* 1986.
32. *Hazelwood School District v. Kuhlmeier* 1988.
33. *Keefe v. Adams* 2016, at 530.
34. Student Press Law Center 2017.
35. Ross 2017.
36. Jaschik 2017.
37. Kaplan Test Prep 2017.
38. Inside Higher Ed and Gallup 2017.
39. Clinedinst and Koranteng 2017.
40. Moody 2018.
41. National Association for College Admission Counseling 2015.
42. Lytle 2011.
43. Indiana University 2016.
44. Georgetown University n.d.
45. Waite and Wheeler 2016.
46. Johnson 2011.
47. University of Salford 2017.
48. Hanover Research 2014.

2

SOCIAL MEDIA STRATEGIES IN ACADEMIC SERVICES

The previous chapter examined how universities are integrating social media into their admissions and enrollment strategies. It is now time to explore how universities are incorporating these online technologies into their academic services. After all, attracting students is one thing; retaining them is quite another. Academic services have become a tremendously important part of a student's world on campus, and technology has affected the manner in which they are delivered to today's college student.

Today's academic services include freshman orientation and first-year programs, advising, tutoring, and mentoring. This chapter reviews the development of academic services on campus, with an emphasis on the ways that new social media tools are being used to address long-standing student and university concerns. In doing so, it offers some observations about key strategies and concepts that will help student affairs professionals effectively incorporate social media into their student program strategies.

STUDENT RETENTION AND THE RISE OF ACADEMIC SERVICES

Historically, student retention was not a key priority for universities. Students enrolled in classes and were assigned grades based on their performance with the understanding that they had a "right to fail." Many universities did not even bother tracking dropout rates since there seemed to be an endless supply of students and resources. As budget surpluses vanished and competition for students increased, this approach to student achievement became untenable.

A 2009 study found that less than 60 percent of the students entering four-year colleges graduate within six years. Graduation rates were particularly low for minority students and those from poor families.[1] Another study discovered that about half of those who drop out do so during their freshman year, with many leaving during the first six to eight weeks on campus.[2] This costs universities financially in the form of lost tuition revenue and increased recruiting costs (to replace lost students).[3]

It is also important to remember that attrition is not distributed evenly among the student body. As noted above, low-income and minority students have lower graduation rates. Not only is retention an issue of fiscal concern for postsecondary schools facing budgetary constraints, but it is also an issue directly related to equity and fairness in higher education. Accrediting agencies, potential donors, and governmental authorities are increasingly expecting universities to document their efforts to reduce student attrition, particularly with at-risk populations. This issue is now so important that college presidents regularly rank student retention as one of the greatest challenges for universities.[4]

Higher-education professionals are beginning to understand the factors that are important for student attrition. Studies show that environmental factors are more influential on student learning and personal development than structural variables such as institution size, prestige, and control (i.e., public or private). What matters is the nature of the experiences students have after matriculation, including the extent of their active involvement in the academic and social systems of their institutions.[5]

Students do not succeed just by virtue of being on campus. They need to become integrated into the campus community. Academic services can help by focusing on student satisfaction with the college experience, effective educational decision making and career planning, awareness and use of campus support services, interaction with faculty outside the classroom, and effective advising, mentoring, and tutoring.

Student commitment to educational and career goals is associated with retention and degree completion.[6] Research suggests that three out of every four freshmen are unsure or tentative about their career choice.[7] Many who enter college with a declared major change their mind at least once before they graduate.[8] While a certain amount of indecisiveness is to be expected as students mature and explore their options, it can also signal confusion, procrastination, or premature decision making due to students' lack of self-reflection and understanding of the relationship between their coursework and their intended career.[9] Research suggests that prolonged indecision about academic major and career goals is correlated with student attrition.[10]

Student use of campus support services also has a demonstrably positive impact on retention given that these services improve both academic performance and self-efficacy.[11] However, research shows that support services are underused by students, particularly the ones who need them the most.[12] At-risk students are less likely to recognize that they are experiencing academic difficulty and are more reluctant to seek help when they do.[13] In light of such findings, institutions are increasingly delivering academic support "intrusively" by initiating contact with students rather than waiting for students to seek help.[14]

Student-faculty interaction outside the classroom has also been found to positively affect student retention.[15] The effect of out-of-class interaction is particularly powerful for students who are prone to withdraw.[16] Such interactions exert the most positive impact when they involve discussions of students' academic interests and career plans.[17]

For similar reasons, student advising, mentoring, and tutoring are all viewed as tools for promoting student retention.[18] These tools are aimed at increasing students' sense of personal significance.[19] The availability of exemplary, caring role models is particularly important for the retention and success of first-generation college students as well as disadvantaged and minority students.[20] One of the principal challenges for institutions is figuring out how to implement advising, mentoring, and tutoring programs on a large-scale basis given that such efforts are traditionally built on dyadic (one-to-one) relationships.[21]

With the goal of strengthening these factors and conditions, colleges and universities across the board have focused more of their attention on academic services. These services include orientation and first-year experiences as well as student advising, mentoring, and tutoring. In turn, student affairs professionals tasked with these efforts are increasingly leveraging sites like Facebook, Twitter, Instagram, and Vine to accomplish their objectives. The goal of this chapter is to provide some context, guidance, and inspiration for doing so.

PREARRIVAL, ORIENTATION, AND THE FIRST-YEAR EXPERIENCE

The process of initiating and integrating newly admitted students into the academic, cultural, and social climate of the university takes place in three phases: prearrival, orientation, and the first-year experience. Social media can be a strategic asset during each phase when student affairs professionals deliberately incorporate them into their communication strategies. The key is to understand the challenges and opportunities that arise due to the nature of each phase.

The Prearrival Phase

Once prospective students accept the university's offer of admission, they are in the prearrival phase. During the prearrival phase, students and their families are full of trepidation and excitement about the life changes that accompany going off to college. Questions abound as parents try to make sure that their sons and daughters have all the material things they will need to be comfortable and successful in their new surroundings. Incoming freshmen (and their parents) vacillate between pride, eagerness, and hope on one hand and worry, anxiety, and fear on the other. While some degree of uncertainty is inevitable for families, colleges and universities can take proactive steps to mitigate these feelings.

It is nearly impossible to overstate the impact that social media has had on this juncture in students' lives. Students increasingly turn to social media to connect with each other and seek answers to questions about life on campus. For example, as soon as room assignments are announced, reaching out to one's roommate on Facebook is now common practice. Doing so helps to relieve some of the anxiety and stress of coordinating a living arrangement between strangers. What used to be accomplished with a telephone call or a letter can now be done more quickly and thoroughly online.

Many students join relevant Facebook pages and groups as soon as they are admitted in order to begin requesting and sharing information with their fellow classmates. These online networks are often created and maintained by students without any express authorization or coordination with university officials. For instance, University of Alabama Class of 2021 is a student-created Facebook group with nearly seven thousand members who are encouraged to post questions, advice, and information regarding school and college life. The page averages more than ten posts per day, but the university does not control or contribute to the content that appears on the page.

Recognizing this as a missed opportunity to establish a meaningful and enduring communication channel with student cohorts, universities are increasingly creating such Facebook groups and pages themselves. Case in point: University of Iowa admissions staff maintains a University of Iowa Class of 2021 Facebook page with nearly three thousand members. Some universities, including the University of Minnesota, have extended this practice to other social networks, such as Snapchat.[22] These networks enable staff to provide incoming students with important dates, relevant information, and campus news. The content posted on the page can evolve to reflect the changing needs and interests of the cohort as they proceed through their four years of college.

Given that anyone on Facebook can create and title a new group, these university-sanctioned pages often compete with unofficial pages bearing the exact same name. In addition to the aforementioned staff-run University of Iowa Class of 2021 Facebook group, there are seven other University of Iowa Class of 2021 groups with memberships ranging from as few as one member to as many as 1,800. These groups are presumably created and maintained by students, though few explicitly say so.

Unlike their authorized counterparts, unauthorized pages and groups often devolve over time as group members deviate from the intended purpose of the group and attempt to leverage the established network for other purposes, such as subleasing apartments, selling used furniture, or seeking out roommates. Unauthorized pages and groups are typically harmless, despite representing a missed opportunity (or friendly competition) for the university. However, some may be seeking to mimic authorized networks for nefarious purposes.

In 2008, college admissions officers started noticing that individuals lacking any connection to their institutions were creating Facebook groups built around their incoming classes. Individuals who joined the group were sent spam messages about a roommate-matching service that cost up to $9.95. The service matched potential roommates based on their responses to a series of survey questions. The students could then contact the university's housing office to request living together in a residence hall. The service had no affiliation or relationship to the universities.

Brad J. Ward, who then worked in the admissions office at Butler University, helped trace the accounts to a startup company called MatchU, founded by Justin Gaither. The universities fought back and had Gaither's sites shut down.[23] However, their victory was short-lived. In 2010, another company founded by Gaither called URoomSurf set up unauthorized Facebook groups for the incoming class of 2015 at more than 150 colleges, including New York University, Middlebury, Wesleyan, and the University of Texas. Each page bore the school's logo as well as descriptions like "Welcome Middlebury Class of 2015" but no reference to URoomSurf, who was sending these groups' members spam about its services.[24] Such recurring instances suggest that fighting back against these types of deceptive marketing practices takes constant vigilance and due diligence.

When proactively incorporated into student affairs strategies, social media can be a key tool for answering students' questions about how to best prepare for the challenges of college life. For example, the Office of Housing, Dining, and Residential Living at Indiana University of Pennsylvania used its Facebook page to promote a list of "Hawks Housing Hints" to help students prepare for life on campus.[25] Similarly,

ACADEMIC SERVICES

Marist College created a Pinterest board full of decorating tips and advice for adjusting to life in the residence halls.[26]

Universities need not produce such content by themselves. They can also help new students prepare for college life prior to their arrival on campus by using social media to solicit advice for incoming freshmen from upperclassmen, faculty, alumni, and parents. For instance, Appalachian State sent out such a request on Facebook and then followed up by compiling the responses into a "Top Five Suggestions" list, which they also posted on Facebook.[27] At Loyola Marymount University, faculty and staff were photographed with a whiteboard containing their advice to new students. The pictures were then uploaded to an album on Facebook titled "Words of Wisdom for #LMU18 Class."[28] The content produced by faculty, students, alumni, and parents in response to such requests is often a perfect blend of humor, helpful tips, and heartfelt sentimentality.

Universities can also create Facebook "events" that cater to incoming freshmen. For example, Morehouse College created a series of events on Facebook called "Morehouse Mondays," wherein administrators and staff from Admissions, Financial Aid, and Student Life participated in live chat sessions.[29] These online events enabled admitted students and their families to get answers to specific questions.

These social media efforts, which often continue right up to the next phase of student integration, can help reduce the stress and anxiety of moving away from home and living in cramped quarters with strangers. In his position as associate director for news and content strategy at the University of Portland, Joe Kuffner put out a request for help on Facebook. Those who responded were sent a poster board sign with the University of Portland logo along the top with instructions to write an inspiring message to incoming students and post it on the major roads and highways leading to Portland to be seen on the day of orientation. As a result of Kuffner's efforts, hundreds of alumni put up encouraging messages for students and their families traveling to campus.[30]

Freshman Orientation

The second phase of new student integration, referred to as "freshman orientation," typically takes place for one or two days on campus during the summer. During this time, new students meet with an adviser and register for classes, take a campus tour, and participate in games and activities designed to make them feel comfortable and excited about coming to campus in the fall.

At one point the question was widely asked, why bother with freshman orientation at all? If freshmen are adults, they should be responsible for their own education. While this Spartan approach may sound good in theory, research has consistently shown the value of orientation programs.[31] They used to be centered on "fun and games," but they have expanded considerably to the degree that they sometimes leave parents and students with a bewildering amount of information.

All orientation efforts are designed to help freshmen make the transition from one environment to another and increase the likelihood that they will be successful college students. Traditionally, these programs have involved face-to-face and small group meetings with advisers, faculty members, residence hall staff, and other academic affairs professionals as per student interest (e.g., Greek life, study abroad, intramural activities). Social media can now provide tools to supplement these traditional freshman orientation activities.

From the minute students arrive on campus, universities strive to make their orientation a social media event. While social media is still used to respond to inquiries and push out announcements during this phase of student integration, the emphasis shifts from information to exhibitionism. The goal is to get students excited about coming to college by showcasing students *being* excited about college. These instances are shared not only among orientation participants but also with other audiences across social media outlets.

Central to this process is the creation and advertising of unique hashtags to be used across multiple social media networks during freshman orientation. Examples include #SJSUfrosh (San Jose State University) and #wmOrientation (William & Mary). Hashtags such as these are featured on nearly every T-shirt, sign, brochure, and online post related to freshman orientation. University administrators refer to them in their speeches, and student orientation leaders promote them for every activity. The creation and advertising of these hashtags has become key to successfully implementing the remainder of the orientation media strategy, which is built on creating and capturing the excitement of entering college.

These hashtags create social media channels that enable university officials and attendees to communicate with each other. They also enable universities to solicit engagement and student-created content. For example, San Jose State University posted the following message on Twitter: "Hey new Spartans, tag orientation pics today w/ #SJSUfrosh to be featured on #SJSU's Twitter."[32] Student affairs professionals then monitored the hashtag on Facebook, Twitter, and Instagram to discover new pictures to share on their official accounts on these networks.

Some universities even create interactive displays during this phase with the express purpose of generating content to be shared on social media. For instance, the University of Portland erected life-sized letters, P-L-O-T-S, in the main quad. The giant letters were spaced in such a way that students could stand between the P and the L to effectively serve as the "I" in Pilots, which is the athletic nickname for the University of Portland. This simple and inexpensive setup resulted in hundreds of photographs posted and shared across multiple social media platforms by orientation attendees.[33]

Universities have also found ways to solicit videos from orientation participants. During orientation at the University of New Hampshire, student affairs professionals used Vine to capture and share six-second videos of incoming students introducing themselves to the Wildcat community. The university featured these recordings on its website and on its official Facebook, Twitter, and Pinterest accounts.[34]

Move-In Day

Between the second and third phases of student integration comes move-in day. While there is some excitement involved, there can also be a considerable amount of drudgery. Students and parents make trip after trip with all the material things that the student will need to be successful. Things must be unpacked and assembled. Move-in day can be a long day for everyone: students, parents, and residence hall staff.

Historically, move-in day was not an event for universities in the most generic sense. It was merely a logistical issue, with lots of people on campus and additional personnel required to manage them. This is no longer the case. Today, it is not uncommon to see returning students, staff, faculty members, and even college administrators participating in move-in day. It is now viewed as a major event—a celebration of the arrival of new students to campus.

Today's student affairs professionals are poised to capture and share the excitement of move-in day on social media. The event is often given its own hashtag (e.g., #UNCAvlMoveIn2015 at the University of North Carolina Asheville), though it is not uncommon for hashtags created for freshman orientation and first-year experience to accompany the move-in day hashtag. Just as before, these hashtags enable universities to solicit, create, and curate online posts.

The University of New Hampshire provides a shining example of how to do so. It used its social media accounts to request that incoming freshmen post photographs of themselves packing, traveling, and moving with the hashtags #IBelieveInUNH and #UNH20. Students' photographs were reposted on the university's official Twitter account, which gained 198 new followers by the end of move-in day. Student affairs professionals even released a limited move-in day geofilter for Snapchat users located near the residence halls. Students were given the chance to win a T-shirt with #IBelieveInUNH printed on it for using the filter and move-in day hashtags. Within six hours, the geofilter had been used 665 times with posts garnering 38,728 views.[35]

The content curated on these sites can be showcased again at the end of students' college experience. During graduation ceremonies, universities routinely feature photographs and videos captured and shared on social media four years previous during freshman orientation and move-in day. This lends to the sentimentality and sense of accomplishment felt by students and their families.

The First-Year Experience

The prearrival phase, orientation phase, and move-in day can be rather intense for students and their families. Each is short, packed with energy and emotion, and contains an overwhelming amount of information. There is little time for students to digest these experiences before they find themselves on campus and attending their first class. The third phase of student integration, typically referred to as the first-year experience, is a more comprehensive approach to socialization efforts that takes place during students' first two semesters of college.[36]

During the 1960s and 1970s, three factors combined to increase the realization that freshmen needed some structured assistance to become successfully assimilated into the college environment. First, the number of first-generation college students increased significantly. This group lacked socialization skills because their parents, who never went to college, were unable to help them know what to expect. Second, college curriculum became more diverse and complicated, leaving many students in need of assistance to navigate their programs of study. Finally, the existing peer culture during this period often deprived freshmen of the experience older students had.[37]

First-year programs have now become so common that there is a National Resource Center for the First-Year Experience and Students in Transition at the University of South Carolina. This center provides research in the field, resources for faculty and professional staff, awards for institutions demonstrating excellence in first-year programming, and even courses on effectively using digital tools in first-year seminars.[38] The center serves as a resource for centralizing the ever-increasing amount of research on orientation and the first-year experience.

Rather than consisting of a single program, the first-year experience typically encompasses a total campus approach to helping students navigate larger issues. These include forming friendships, developing study habits, using university resources, and a host of other issues that affect students. As such, the use of social media shifts from information and exhibitionism to relationship building and personal development.

This shift coincides with students' newfound independence during the first weeks of the new school year. Those who struggle to form relationships with others are at a higher risk of failure given that peer groups help mitigate the struggles students face. Alienated from the peer groups they formed in high school, freshmen entering college can quickly succumb to social anxiety and loneliness.

According to social-comparison research and social psychology, young people tend to overestimate their own intelligence and capabilities. But when it comes to friendships, a study found that nearly half (48 percent) of freshmen assumed that other freshmen had more close friends than they did. Estimating that others had more exciting social lives was consistent across gender and ethnicity and was true whether a student had attended a local high school or migrated from out of town.[39]

Given that many users cultivate online personas that are happier and more engaged than they are in real life, social media has the potential to exacerbate this "compare-and-despair" phenomenon. The challenge for student affairs professionals is to counterbalance this by using social media to make students' self-perceived friendship gap seem small and surmountable. Strategies for doing so begin as soon as freshmen move into the residence halls, where living arrangements have a direct impact on social integration.[40]

Student affairs professionals can use social media to mediate the first-year experience by intentionally providing students information that includes references to the difficulties faced by many freshmen who are away from home for the first time. Social media can, and should, be used to celebrate the new experiences that first-time college students have, but it can also be used to regularly remind students that they may not be the only ones who are experiencing difficulties with loneliness, depression, or adjusting to the social and academic rigors of college life. These types of messages might be particularly well received when they come from residence hall assistants, many of whom are upper-level students themselves.

The intentional combination of academic and cocurricular efforts that characterize the first-year experience is often accompanied by a required "freshman seminar" course. Like any other course, such a seminar will have a corresponding site on the university's learning management system, such as Blackboard or Canvas. Research suggests that the creation of a corresponding social media outlet, such as a course Facebook page, can give new students the choice to participate in conversations about their challenges in a more familiar, more porous, and less formal setting than the walled-off community of a learning management system.[41] This can be particularly helpful to new students whose challenges may include navigating such systems.

Getting students to campus and getting them successfully integrated into the campus community is one of the more important challenges facing colleges and universities. If students leave campus without a degree, the time and resources that universities spend in recruiting and enrolling students is largely for naught. Perhaps more importantly, students who leave college may never return, a decision that can have long-lasting financial and emotional consequences.

Social media tools are ideally suited to help students make the transition from one physical and social community to another. They help facilitate the flow of information, which can be overwhelming for new students, and provide an additional avenue for meeting new friends, joining groups, and participating in new activities. They can simultaneously allow students to revel in their own unique experiences as they go off to college and help them feel that they are becoming part of a larger community of students.

STUDENT ADVISING, MENTORING, AND TUTORING

In many important ways, academic advising goes hand in hand with the orientation and first-year attempts at building community. While the focus there may be primarily on *social* community, academic advising helps students become a successful part of the *academic* community on campus. It is important to note that quality advising, like social community building, has been linked to increased student retention.[42] They reinforce one another to help students be successful in all aspects of campus life.

Academic advising requires maintaining close contact with a student to assess and enhance the quality of that student's educational experience. While faculty members once occupied this role, the duration and depth of relationships built in the classroom, even in small classes, make such an expectation unrealistic in modern higher education.[43] Rather, it requires the creation of systematic advising programs wherein dedicated advisers establish a stable, ongoing relationship with individual students and maintain continuous contact with them throughout their college experience.

The Importance of Academic Advising

Academic advising has been in existence, in one form or another, since the inception of higher education in the United States.[44] In the nation's first colleges, faculty members—largely consisting of clergymen training their pupils to be clergymen themselves—resided with their students to ensure their moral and intellectual development.[45] While college faculty began to shed their paternalism as America declared and fought for its independence from England, leaving students responsible for their own moral development, the proliferation of colleges throughout the nineteenth century was accompanied by the emergence of faculty advising groups tasked with vocational guidance.[46]

During World War I and World War II, universities strengthened their advising programs and began using occupational aptitude assessments as an advising tool, a practice borrowed from the U.S. Army, who used industrial psychology practices to place recruits into specific occupations based on their skills and intelligence.[47] The demand for advising increased as baby boomers flocked to college campuses during the 1960s and 1970s. During this time, academic advising became increasingly concerned with addressing issues related to social justice, access, usefulness, and accountability.[48] Nearly fifty years later, universities are still dedicated to preparing their students for the job market while simultaneously addressing these larger issues.

Advising on college campuses can take a variety of forms, which may be dependent on the size and type of college. Some colleges use faculty to advise students. The advantage of this model is that students may have a better opportunity to build relationships with faculty members, relationships that foster academic success. Faculty members are also content experts in their fields and are perhaps better prepared to explain how and why programs of study are organized the way they are.

But many faculty members think such tasks are below their station, often complaining, "I didn't get a PhD in [their chosen field] to fill out students' degree maps." Another drawback to this advising arrangement is the fact that faculty are often less tech savvy than their students. While faculty are becoming more adept at incorporating technology into their classes, this does not necessarily transfer to the myriad of specialized ways that technology is used in the advising process.

Other colleges have professional advising staff. The benefit of this is that these individuals have the time and expertise to address student issues that the faculty-mentor model may not. The drawback to this approach is that hiring more professional staff costs money and resources that cannot then be spent directly educating students. Most colleges employ some version of this model, but some retain the faculty-mentor model or use some type of hybrid.

Today's adviser performs several roles: a guide to help students adhere to formal policies and administrative protocol, a referral agent who connects students to campus support systems, a confidante students can rely on for advice and guidance, and an advocate for student rights.[49] Advisers' efforts in these roles can be characterized as either prescriptive or developmental.[50] The type of online technology used by advisers is dependent on the type of effort being undertaken.[51]

Prescriptive advising consists of providing students with concrete answers, much like a doctor prescribes medicine to be taken by his or her patients. This can include responding to student questions via email, plugging courses into online degree-mapping programs, using equivalency websites to assess transfer courses, and directing students to .edu websites to ascertain information about core curriculum requirements, course restrictions, degree tracks, and other specific institutional information. These prescriptive online technologies enable students to problem-solve autonomously, which is an important area of development for students.[52] However, they can also result in one-sided conversations wherein advisers merely discuss various requirements without assessing students' broader needs and difficulties.[53]

Developmental advising, on the other hand, focuses on empowering students to become more self-aware of their interests, abilities, values, and priorities. This type of advising has become increasingly popular in recent years, but it also exacerbates two key advising issues: time and caseload. Developmental advising takes more time since interactions with each student are usually longer and sometimes more frequent as well.[54] There is also evidence to show that this more interactive (or "intrusive") type of advising contributes to student retention. While this approach is often more popular with students, it becomes difficult to achieve when each full-time adviser has a caseload that numbers well into the hundreds.[55]

Rather than providing students with technological resources that lead them to concrete answers, developmental advising guides them to resources that encourage self-reflection and personal development. Social media are becoming increasingly important in developmental advising, both as a tool for the creation of digital identities as well as for their potential for digitized development.

Using Digital Tools in Advising

Communicating

Technology is already widely used in advising settings in most universities. Websites, student information systems, degree audit programs, webinars, and career guidance programs are all quite common. Social media adds yet another tool to the digital toolbox. Blogs can be used to post information on meetings, agendas, and events.[56] Students can also "meet" with advisers via Skype and receive information through Facebook sites and Twitter feeds. Providing these additional means of communication can be advantageous for students, particularly those who are more comfortable with online communication than they are with face-to-face communication.

While some students prefer the opportunity to use technology in the advising process, most still prefer some degree of face-to-face interaction.[57] Physically sitting and talking with their adviser can help students (and their advisers) feel reassured they are on the right path. This is why students are often told that social media is not a replacement for comprehensive meetings with advisers.

Professionalization

Prior to college, many young people use online technologies primarily as a social instrument to play games or interact with friends. When they arrive on campus their relationship with technology changes as they reconceive these tools in light of their educational and professional goals. They begin to recognize the value of the various presentations, personas, and constructions of an individual in the online space.[58] Likewise, they gain a greater appreciation of social media's ability to serve as a means of acquiring information about nearly *anything*.

Social media allows individuals to present themselves online and then reflect on how such a presentation affects their self-perception as well as others' perceptions. In doing so, these technologies help college students explore and make sense of their identities.[59] Advisers can foster student development by guiding individuals to appropriate platforms (e.g., using LinkedIn to establish a polished, professional identity) and encouraging them to reflect on how their behavior on social media might be perceived by peers, professors, and potential employers.

Proper developmental advising depends on acknowledging that how students use social media changes over time. As young adults move toward independence, they often exhibit approval-seeking behaviors. On social media, the "likes" (or "favorites") and "shares" act as a form of external validation that what one is expressing is valid, interesting, or important. Students develop self-authorship as they proceed through college, relying less on external definition by others and more on internal definition wherein they establish their own self-concept based on what is important to them.[60] Throughout this transition, advisers must communicate with students to ensure they are internalizing values and goals that are consistent with the mission of the university and the norms of their chosen academic field.

The process of growth and self-learning that occurs in the complex and overlapping contexts of digital technologies also provides advisers with an opportunity to show students how to become more self-sufficient.[61] Advisers can help students use social media to become aware of new information and opportunities that align with their interests. Advisers can also help students use these tools to develop new connections with like-minded people with whom they can share information and learning experiences. These advising efforts are time-consuming, but they can result in more resilient students who require less advising as they progress toward graduation.

Mentoring

Mentors are professional guides who nurture and promote the learning and success of their protégés.[62] The terms *adviser* and *mentor* are often used synonymously, particularly at institutions where advisers have embraced their role in developmental advising, but many universities have created robust mentoring programs separate from academic advisers. Faculty members often serve as mentors in these programs, providing more experience and expertise in students' area of study than academic advisers.

A growing body of research has examined the benefits of mentoring in educational settings.[63] These benefits can be characterized as informational (i.e., the transfer of information and subject matter), psychosocial (i.e., enhancement of self-esteem, confidence, and risk-taking), and instrumental (i.e., opportunities and experiences).[64] Unfortunately, informal or naturally occurring mentoring relationships are not equitably available, particularly to female[65] and minority[66] students. The creation of formal mentoring programs helps level the playing field for students who might find it difficult to initiate mentoring relationships on their own.

Along with the creation of the Internet and large-scale adoption of online technologies such as email came e-mentoring programs. These programs did not replace traditional face-to-face advising but rather provided additional mentoring opportunities that otherwise would not exist. Studies show that e-mentoring can deliver many of the same informational, psychosocial, and instrumental benefits as face-to-face mentoring.[67]

E-mentoring provides students with several advantages compared to face-to-face mentoring, including attenuation of status differences, the ability to participate without the stigma of taking part in a remediation program, and the ability to be matched with mentors outside of one's geographic region and established networks.[68] However, e-mentoring can also suffer from its means of delivery. Electronic communications have fewer reinforcement cues that encourage the maintenance of a relationship.[69] One of the challenges for universities is getting students who sign up for e-mentoring programs to follow through and respond to email messages from program staff and e-mentoring partners.

Universities have attempted to address these challenges by experimenting with alternatives to the traditional mentoring dyad between mentor and protégé, including communal models and group e-mentoring.[70]

Approaches based on peer mentoring have also been successful. Wilkes University in Wilkes-Barre, Pennsylvania, started an award-winning e-mentoring program that connects upperclassmen with incoming students via a variety of electronic and face-to-face means.[71] It is designed to provide incoming students with information and ease the transition to college life.

Alumni can also serve as mentors and help orient new students to the rigors of college life. Phoenix College, a part of the Maricopa Community College system, uses Snapchat to keep mentors and mentees in constant communication.[72] Another variation of this is the It Takes a Village Challenge (#ITAVChallenge). The program, created by Jasmine and Eric Cooper, uses social media to recruit successful African American college graduates willing to "adopt" a graduating high school senior who will be attending their alma mater, supplying them with some financial assistance (e.g., textbook money) but more importantly a role model that they can keep in contact with as they transition to the college environment.[73]

INTERNATIONAL STUDENT SERVICES

According to the Institute of International Education, there are more than one million international students enrolled in U.S. colleges and universities.[74] These students often face difficulties adjusting to their new surroundings and academic environment. Complex legal requirements, as well as language and cultural differences, can amplify the challenges associated with supporting and integrating these students. To address these challenges, universities have established international student services offices dedicated to assisting with issues related to logistics, academics, and social support.

Many of these students are unaware of the organizations, spaces, and programs that are available to help them or are hesitant to use them. Cultural stigmas can exacerbate international students' reluctance to seek help when they need it. This helps explain why student affairs professionals working in these offices have increasingly turned to online technologies such as websites, email, and social media to actively reach out to international students. These technologies help lower the barriers to seeking and receiving various types of support.

The global popularity of sites like Facebook, Twitter, Instagram, and YouTube makes it more likely that international students are already using these platforms, making them well suited for supplementing traditional means of addressing the needs of international students.[75] It is not surprising that international student services offices maintain accounts on one or more of these platforms. Social media have become an important tool for international students' "everyday life information seeking."[76]

Communicating Logistical Information

The first priority of student affairs professionals is to support students in obtaining and maintaining legal status. This includes guiding them through necessary paperwork and explaining visa issues as they pertain to jobs, internships, and postgraduation residency in the United States. Other logistical issues include helping international students prepare for weather throughout the year, teaching them to navigate using local transportation systems such as bus and subway lines, and informing them of financial resources. Likewise, international students are made aware of the institution's health and wellness facilities as well as the safety measures provided by campus and local police.

Universities have traditionally relied on mandatory orientation sessions and a plethora of printed materials to communicate logistical information. International student services offices often leverage mandatory orientation and advising sessions to promote other opportunities for international students to receive relevant logistical information. These opportunities include lawyers invited to deliver workshops on maintaining legal status, guided tours on and off campus, and meet-and-greet gatherings with key university personnel.

Social media platforms provide new means of communicating logistical information. Facebook, in particular, is useful for this purpose given that page administrators can create *events* complete with a picture (or video) as well as a name, location, date, time, and description. Once it is created, individuals who have "liked" the page can click on the event title and choose "Interested," "Going," or "Can't Go" from a dropdown menu. Unless the user chooses the latter, the event will be placed on the individual's events calendar, and he or she will receive updates about the event as well as periodic reminders prior to its occurrence.

This function makes it easy to remind students of important requirements and deadlines. For instance, the Office of International Student Services at Texas A&M University routinely created events on its Facebook page to remind international students planning on traveling outside the United States to get their travel signature on forms and have them processed.[77]

At the University of Wisconsin–Madison, International Student Services frequently created events on its Facebook page to promote workshops aimed at helping international students become aware of employment visa options.[78] These events, and the periodic reminders pushed by the system, can be a tremendous asset to international students, who may find the amount of important information being shared with them to be overwhelming at times.

Academic Support

In addition to helping international students deal with logistical issues, student affairs professionals are also responsible for helping these students adjust to their new academic environment. This includes helping international students understand expectations regarding classroom behavior and academic integrity as well as ensuring they are aware of various support services across campus, including physical and mental health services, library services, tutoring programs, and writing centers. Universities have experimented with several programs and services to address these issues with the goal of not only informing international students about relevant information but also encouraging them to become more involved on campus.

Some universities implement a "buddy program" that pairs international students with an American peer who has volunteered to provide guidance throughout the semester. Others, such as Stanford University, have organized luncheons where faculty members lead discussions with small groups of international students about opportunities for academic and cocurricular involvement. And some institutions, like Iowa State University, have developed leadership programs aimed at building international students' leadership skills, including public speaking, project management, networking, team building, conflict management, and time and resource management. These leadership programs are developed with the goal of increasing the number of leadership roles in extracurricular and cocurricular organizations occupied by international students.[79]

Student affairs professionals use hashtags to market these types of academic resources. These hashtags enable student affairs professionals to target multiple audiences (e.g., graduate students, international students, and business majors) while providing a unique channel to communicate information about disparate programs and events. For instance, the graduate school at the University of South Carolina used #GRADprofdev to promote a series of events aimed at providing professional development opportunities for graduate students. The Office of International Student Services cross-promoted these opportunities on its own Facebook page using the same hashtag, which not only made international students aware of the events but also enabled them to join the conversation by tagging their own Facebook posts with #GRADprofdev.

STUDY ABROAD PROGRAMS

Study abroad programs provide students with opportunities for valuable and enriching experiences while they temporarily live and study in a foreign country. Research suggests a number of positive student outcomes that can result from the facilitation of study abroad programs, including improved retention and academic performance. Research indicates that more than 90 percent of colleges and universities in the

United States offer study abroad programs, with more than 250,000 students participating in these programs annually.[80]

Social media has also proven to be a powerful promotional tool for universities' study abroad programs. Traditionally, universities present study abroad information by destination or discipline. Social media can help facilitate a third advertising strategy based on sending tailored messages to segmented audiences.

Students can be motivated to study abroad for a variety of reasons. Career-oriented students may pursue study abroad programs for the value they add to their résumé or because they want to live and work abroad after graduation. Other students may be more interested in traveling and sightseeing. Others may be motivated by a desire to connect with their heritage or visit family living abroad. Universities can strategically use social media to reach these various segments of potential study abroad participants.

―――

For example, the International Programs and Services office at the University of Minnesota Duluth targets career-oriented students by using LinkedIn to advertise the unique academic opportunities within a particular field that exist outside the United States.[81] The Office of International Programs and Services at Pace University uses Instagram to showcase foreign locales, landmarks, and activities in an effort to target students interested in traveling and sightseeing.[82] Similarly, it is not uncommon for such offices to target heritage seekers by advertising study abroad programs on various multicultural student groups' Facebook pages.

Social media can aid in advertising study abroad programs in other ways. Student affairs professionals can use social media to connect students who want to study outside the United States with students who currently are or who have already done so. At Indiana University–Purdue University Indianapolis students participating in study abroad programs can apply to be social media student ambassadors, documenting their experiences and answering questions from those who might be interested in replicating them.[83] The International Studies Department at Texas A&M requested that students tag their study abroad photos on Instagram with #INTSabroad so they could be featured on their own social media accounts.[84] Similarly, Brigham Young University produced an international spin-off of its #MyViewFromBYU Instagram stories, allowing five study abroad participants to take over the university's Instagram account to document a typical day of immersing themselves in their host country's language, culture, food, and transportation.[85]

Traditional means of preparing students for study abroad include mandatory meetings and folders full of forms, waivers, brochures, maps, and handouts. It is common for universities to host information sessions and panel discussions featuring former study abroad participants and international students from the host country. While these strategies have remained a staple of predeparture planning in the twenty-first century, they are now being supplemented with practices that leverage the popularity of social media.

The ubiquity of mobile phone service means that sojourners have access to social media technologies nearly anywhere in the world. These technologies provide universities with new means of preparing students to study abroad as well as keeping them safe, informed, and engaged while they are outside the United States. They also provide universities with valuable opportunities to advertise their study abroad programs to other students.

During the predeparture phase, students can become overwhelmed by the amount of information provided to them about the study abroad experience. Student affairs professionals can use social media to help remind students to obtain passports, fill out important paperwork, register for credit hours, and fulfill a number of other obligations. These technologies also provide an outlet for tips and suggestions that might receive less attention during traditional predeparture planning sessions. Student affairs professionals can also help students use social media to do research about their host countries and connect with local students before they arrive.

Social media has made it much easier for universities to maintain contact with their students while they are out of the country. These technologies offer students new opportunities to chronicle and share their study abroad experience. Student affairs professionals can also use sites like Facebook and Twitter to inform study abroad participants of events and points of interest in the host country during their visit or issue safety warnings during natural and man-made disasters.

While social media can help universities keep their students safe and informed during their study abroad, there is a concern among many higher-education professionals that these technologies may be diminishing the immersive nature of study abroad programs.[86] This is because social media makes it easier for individuals to be physically present in one space but mentally present in another.[87] Furthermore, social media can exacerbate feelings of homesickness and loneliness by reminding students of what they are missing back home. Student affairs professionals can mitigate these drawbacks by using social media to promote immersive activities as well as encouraging students to use social media to explore their host country's culture and connect with its residents.

Universities are increasingly using social media to prepare students for study abroad programs, communicate with participants while they are outside the United States, and market these programs to individuals with a diverse range of interests. As this trend continues, it is important to step back and consider the unique opportunities and potential pitfalls of doing so. By strategically incorporating these technologies into their study abroad programs, student affairs professionals can more effectively meet student needs and bolster their institution's retention efforts.

CONCLUSION

Gone are the days when students arrived on campus and were just expected to "figure it out." Higher-education professionals now recognize that students and their families often need some form of assistance to become acclimated to the campus environment. This view accounts for the development of academic services on college campuses, particularly in areas that have the greatest impact on retention.

The size and scope of academic services on campus has changed and grown. So, too, have the tools at their disposal. Face-to-face meetings with student affairs professionals, small group meetings, fliers and posters, and advertising campaigns are still used, but they have been supplemented with today's social media tools.

One of the best things about using social media in this capacity is that it allows for students to create their own content, giving them a sense of ownership in the college transition process. However, this process can be a delicate one. Units must be reflective about their abilities and their goals. The benefits are worth it since the more students see themselves as a part of the college community, the more likely they are to become successful college students.

DISCUSSION QUESTIONS

- How is social media being used to integrate students into the university and build a sense of community? How are these approaches being leveraged as each incoming class progresses toward graduation?
- Has the institution had to deal with third parties on social media mirroring or masquerading as a university-sanctioned entity? If so, how has the college dealt with this? Who monitors for such accounts?
- How are student affairs colleagues using digital tools to supplement the mentoring and advising process?
- What is being done to help students develop a professional digital identity? Who plays a role in this process (e.g., staff, faculty, employers)?
- How does the university use social media to assist international students in all facets of university living (e.g., academia, social, communicating back home)?

NOTES

1. Bowen et al. 2009.
2. Noel et al. 1985.
3. Holbrook 1981.
4. Jaschik and Lederman 2017.
5. Pascarella and Terenzini 2005.
6. Wyckoff 1999.
7. Titley and Titley 1980.
8. Gordon 1984.
9. Upcraft, Finney, and Garland 1984.

ACADEMIC SERVICES

10. Astin 1975.
11. Smith, Walter, and Hoey 1992.
12. Knapp and Karabenick 1988.
13. Levin and Levin 1991.
14. Cuseo n.d.
15. Pascarella and Terenzini 1991.
16. Tinto 1975.
17. Terenzini 1986.
18. Walker and Taub 2001.
19. Schlossberg, Lynch, and Chickering 1989.
20. Tinto 1987.
21. Redmond 1990.
22. University of Minnesota 2019.
23. "Campus Overlord" 2010.
24. Steinberg 2010.
25. Indiana University of Pennsylvania 2019.
26. Marist College 2019.
27. Appalachian State University 2019.
28. Loyola Marymount University 2019.
29. Morehouse University 2019.
30. Kuffner 2013.
31. Perigo and Upcraft 1989.
32. San Jose State University 2016.
33. Kuffner 2016.
34. University of New Hampshire 2016.
35. Ibid.
36. Harrington and Orosz 2018.
37. Dwyer 1989.
38. National Resource Center for First-Year Experience and Students in Transition 2019.
39. Whillans et al. 2017.
40. Wilcox, Winn, and Fyvie-Gauld 2005.
41. Jenkins et al. 2012.
42. Crookston 1972.
43. Winston et al. 1984.
44. Gillispie 2003; O'Banion 2020.
45. Gallagher and Demos 1983.
46. Gordon 1992.
47. Gallagher and Demos 1983.
48. Komives and Woodward 1996.
49. Cuseo n.d.

50. Crookston 1994.
51. Underwood and Underwood 2015.
52. Pascarella and Terenzini 2005.
53. Shaffer et al. 2010.
54. Gordon 1994.
55. Jaggars and Karp 2016.
56. University of Buffalo Pre-Law Advising Blog 2018.
57. Gaines 2014.
58. Brown 2016a.
59. Alemán and Wartman 2009.
60. Baxter Magolda 2001.
61. Brown 2016b.
62. Sands et al. 1992.
63. Russell and Adams 1997.
64. Single 2004.
65. Ragins and Cotton 1991.
66. Turner and Thompson 1993.
67. Ensher et al. 2004.
68. Single and Single 2005.
69. Sproull and Kiesler 1992.
70. Packard 2003.
71. Wilkes University 2018.
72. Phoenix College 2018.
73. Dupere 2017.
74. Institute of International Education 2017.
75. Saw et al. 2012.
76. Sin and Kim 2013.
77. Texas A&M University Office of International Student Services 2013.
78. University of Wisconsin International Student Services 2019.
79. Greenberg and Moore 2013.
80. Twombly et al. 2012.
81. University of Minnesota Duluth Study Abroad 2019.
82. Pace University Study Abroad 2019.
83. Indiana University–Purdue University at Indianapolis Study Abroad 2015.
84. Texas A&M University Department of International Studies 2019.
85. McBride 2017.
86. Huesca 2013.
87. Buckingham 2008.

3

SOCIAL MEDIA STRATEGIES FOR STUDENT HEALTH AND WELLNESS

For more than one hundred years, colleges and universities have promoted the physical and mental well-being of their students. The services provided, and the means of providing them, have changed significantly over the years. It is now common for institutions of higher learning to offer comprehensive student health programs that provide a variety of services, including primary medical care, mental health counseling, health education and prevention programs, and disability services. These health programs help students achieve their academic, intellectual, and personal potential by addressing the quality of the learning environment and the overall health of the student body. This chapter examines the complicated relationship between social media and the physical, mental, and social well-being of students.

INSTITUTIONAL EFFORTS TO ATTEND TO THE WELL-BEING OF COLLEGE STUDENTS

The comprehensive student health programs common on college campuses today are a relatively new phenomenon. Prior to the 1860s, students were generally seen as responsible for their own health and were expected to seek aid from medical professionals in surrounding communities. This changed in 1861, when Amherst College created the first comprehensive department of hygiene and physical education, which provided annual examinations and instruction on hygiene and treated student illnesses. Other institutions began seeking ways to address students' physical well-being soon thereafter. By the 1890s, colleges and universities were developing student infirmaries to serve students who were unable to care for themselves, and by the early 1900s formally organized student health services were emerging.[1]

The student health services created in the latter half of the nineteenth century focused on students' physical well-being. Physicians emphasized the importance of proper exercise and a healthy diet for avoiding emotional problems, but counseling services were not available. Aside from mentoring by faculty and clergy, students were left to deal with mental health issues on their own.[2] Things began to change shortly after the turn of the century.

Princeton University established the first dedicated mental health service in 1910 after administrators noted that many well-qualified students were leaving school without completing their degree due to emotional and mental health issues. Over the next two decades, a handful of other institutions followed suit, including the University of Wisconsin (1914), Dartmouth College (1921), and Yale University (1925).[3] Relying primarily on psychiatrists who treated their patients by prescribing medications, these initial programs were decades ahead of the comprehensive mental health and counseling services that began to appear in the 1950s.

Congress passed the Serviceman's Readjustment Act of 1944, more commonly known as the G.I. Bill of Rights, as World War II came to an end. The legislation provided $500 per year to qualified veterans for educational expenses. The legislation resulted in a surge of applications from veterans and a corresponding increase in the number of physically disabled students on campus as well as an increase in the number of students dealing with mental health challenges.

The social and cultural revolution that swept the country in the 1960s forever changed the student health agenda. This era was characterized by political tensions due to civil rights and Vietnam, an increase in drug and alcohol abuse, and the sexual revolution, all of which were manifest in the counterculture that existed on college campuses. As student activists became more vocal in expressing their discontent with campus agencies and services that were not meeting their needs, health centers responded by providing more specialized services, including women's clinics offering gynecologic and contraceptive services as well as new programs designed to address drug and alcohol abuse.

To address students' mental health and emotional well-being, most colleges and universities began using a multidisciplinary staff of psychiatrists, psychologists, and psychiatric social workers. The term *learning disability* also emerged during the 1960s, along with expectations that accommodations and resources be made available for students who suffer from such disabilities. Funding for these services shifted from general university revenues to student fees and separate health insurance coverage.[4]

In the 1970s, federal legislation was passed requiring institutions to provide special education services to students with disabilities. This legislation requires both public and private institutions to consider the applications of disabled students, improve access to campus programs and facilities, and address discrimination on the basis of a disability. It also ended the practice of counseling disabled students into more restrictive majors and careers.[5]

In the 1980s, refinements to the diagnostic categories in the *Diagnostic and Statistical Manual of Psychiatric Disorders*—as well as the addition of various adjustment disorders, eating disorders, and learning disorders—made the manual more applicable to college students. Over the next thirty years, mental health services on college campuses continued to grow in size and sophistication. The rise of personal computing and the advent of the Internet during this time revolutionized the way that institutions collected and stored student data. This allowed colleges and universities to expand their array of services and seek new ways to help disabled students engage in goal-directed, self-regulated, autonomous behavior.[6] The rise of social media presents both new challenges and new opportunities for accomplishing these goals.

THE IMPACT OF SOCIAL MEDIA ON STUDENT WELLNESS

The imperative to address the changing needs of students is once again driving institutions to adapt. The integration of online technologies into nearly every facet of higher education, as well as into students' social lives and daily routines, has had dramatic implications for student affairs professionals tasked with responsibilities related to student wellness. Social media has changed not only the types of issues institutions must address but also how they go about doing so.

Social Media and Accessibility

The Americans with Disabilities Act and Section 504 of the Rehabilitation Act of 1973 mandate equal access to postsecondary institutions (both public and private) for students with disabilities. These laws, which apply to nearly all institutions, prohibit colleges and universities from requiring students to disclose that they have a disability, denying admission based on a student's disability, or excluding students from a particular class, program, or activity because of a disability. They cover any disability that substantially limits one or more major life activity that contributes to the proper functioning of the human body (e.g., seeing, sleeping, hearing, talking, moving) or the functioning of internal organs (e.g., using the bathroom independently).

There are some limits to these requirements. Colleges and universities can refuse to provide accommodations that would put an excessive financial or administrative burden on the institution. They are also not required to provide students with personal attendants, readers, or other devices. As institutions of higher learning have integrated online technologies into their core functions, however, disabled students and their parents expect them to make the appropriate accommodations for their use.

Efforts to accommodate students' accessibility needs have traditionally centered on three broad areas: transportation (e.g., parking privileges, elevator access, assistance traversing campus, ramps into buildings), housing (e.g., first-floor rooms, permission to live in residence halls until graduation), and classroom instruction (e.g., priority registration, provision of note takers, seating accommodations).[7] Today, students and higher-education professionals must grapple with a host of new accessibility challenges brought on by the Internet and the rise of social media. Given that these challenges can be invisible, they are often overlooked by faculty, staff, and administrators who are trying to integrate new technologies into their communication routines.

Social media sites often require some form of authentication, such as transcribing a visual verification code of slanted and distorted letters (e.g., a CAPTCHA system), that make registering for an account incredibly difficult for those with visual impairments or dyslexia. These sites are also rich in images, links, and complex interactions that rely on scripting languages that may not be compatible with accessibility software (e.g., screen-reading programs).[8] To complicate matters further, social media sites routinely change their layouts as new features are introduced.

Student affairs professionals have an obligation to help faculty and staff address these issues in order to make material posted on social media accessible to all students, including those with a disability. Simple practices such as capitalizing the first letter of each word in a hashtag (referred to as "camelbacking") or adding alternative text to images can make a world of difference for the visually impaired. Similarly, adding a caption file or using YouTube's captioning services can make videos more accessible.

A growing number of colleges and universities are highlighting the value of inclusiveness and accessibility, drawing attention to issues faced by various types of disabled students, and advertising the disability services available on campus and in the community. Social media has become a key tool in these efforts. For instance, Cornell University launched a social media campaign aimed at increasing awareness of disability issues and support for an inclusive and accessible environment for disabled students. During each month of the campaign, students, faculty, and staff were featured discussing various disability-related topics, including non-obvious disabilities, the self-identification of disability, and physical and web accessibility. These stories were communicated on the university's website as well as social media platforms using the hashtag #DiversityIncludesDisability.[9]

Social Media and Learning Disabilities

The number of students with some form of learning disability has grown dramatically since the 1960s. This increase may be due to a greater share of disabled students reporting their disability in order to receive accommodations, but it may also be the case that social media is contributing to an increase in the number of students who suffer from a learning disability. For example, research suggests that high-frequency use of social media is associated with the development of symptoms of attention deficit/hyperactivity disorder (ADHD).[10] It is not surprising that the constant stream of status updates, alerts, notifications, and advertisements might disrupt students' concentration and prevent them from staying on task.

Colleges and universities have generally been concerned with providing classroom and testing accommodations for students with learning disabilities. These accommodations are designed to overcome specific barriers encountered because of a student's disability but do little to promote self-advocacy and self-determination. In more recent years, however, student affairs professionals have turned their attention to opportunities that take a more inclusive, holistic approach to student success. This includes e-mentoring programs likes the ones described in chapter 2 as well as guiding students with learning disabilities toward new technologies that can help them address challenges on their own. Given the impossible task of keeping students off of their phones, the most prudent thing to do may be to help students reimagine these machines as more than simply a means of accessing social media.

Smartphones and various applications that run on them enable students to make audio and video recordings, take pictures, transcribe notes, list tasks, create a schedule, and set reminders. Students with learning disabilities can become more organized and improve their study processes by taking advantage of these tools. Student affairs professionals are fond of these technologies because they help students develop self-regulation and leave them feeling more in control of their lives.

Social Media and Physical Health

Though traditional undergraduate students are typically thought to be in generally good health, a growing number are entering college out of shape. Approximately 40 percent of college-aged adults (ages eighteen to twenty-four) are classified as either overweight or obese.[11] These students are at higher risk of suffering from physical and mental health challenges that can be a detriment to their education.

Social media can contribute to a number of factors associated with weight gain and obesity. Some research suggests that social media users are at greater risk of sedentariness, sleep disturbance, and succumbing to the persuasive effects of food marketing.[12] Curbing these behaviors has become an important task for student affairs professionals concerned with student health.

Many colleges and universities have pursued obesity prevention initiatives consisting of programs that educate students about nutrition, promote physical activity, and enable healthy weight management. These programs can be delivered via printed materials, group lectures, personal counseling, and online platforms including websites and social media. Online obesity prevention programs that use social media and email components can prevent weight gain among college freshmen[13] and increase healthy weight management behaviors among all college students.[14] A study of community college students found that those who participated in a technology-centered program called Choosing Healthy Options in College Environments and Settings (CHOICES) were three times more likely to transition to a healthy weight by the end of the trial than those who did not participate.[15]

Using social media to address student health issues like diet and exercise can be tricky. On the one hand, online communities can provide social support and information for users who are engaged in weight-loss activities. Even if they do not interact with other members of the community, they may find it valuable to simply follow institutional accounts that advertise campus resources, obesity experts, and others who are attempting to lose weight.

On the other hand, research suggests that user-generated discourse surrounding the topic of obesity on sites like Twitter and Facebook tends to be dominated by derogatory and misogynistic sentiments.[16] Student affairs professionals need to be prepared to deal with these types of comments when they attempt to use social media to promote proper exercise and diet routines and counter weight-based stereotypes. This speaks to the importance of establishing a policy regarding civil discourse prior to initiating these types of conversations online.

Social Media and Mental Well-being

Counseling centers on college campuses have often been understaffed because the budgets for these services result from historical calculations based on the number of students enrolled and previous rates of students requesting appointments. But recent data suggests the number of college students seeking help for mental health issues is outpacing the growth in enrollment by more than fivefold.[17] Between fall 2009 and spring 2015, counseling center use increased by an average of 30 to 40 percent, but enrollment increased by only 5 percent during this time.[18] This has led many higher-education professionals to declare that colleges and universities are experiencing a mental health crisis.

But what accounts for the increase in student demand for mental health services? Are students simply more willing to discuss their mental health issues, or do these changes reflect a student body suffering from more maladies than in the past? To what extent are these changes related to the rise of smartphones and social media? And what does all of this mean for those tasked with addressing students' mental health challenges? These are some of the most pressing questions in higher education today.

Studies suggest that more students are reporting a wider variety of mental health issues than they have in the past. Anxiety and depression continue to be the most common challenges faced by students, but more students are reporting a lifetime prevalence of "threat-to-self" characteristics.

In 2018, the Center for Collegiate Mental Health at Penn State University's survey of students receiving campus mental health services revealed that 27.8 percent of respondents had engaged in nonsuicidal self-injury, 35.8 percent reported having serious suicidal ideation, and 10.3 percent had attempted suicide. While the majority of college students seeking mental health treatment at campus counseling centers do so only occasionally, the study found that 20 percent of college students seeking mental health treatment were taking up 56 percent of all appointments at campus counseling centers.[19]

The demand for campus mental health services has increased so dramatically that institutions are finding it difficult to handle. With immediate "threat-to-self" issues taking prominence, resources are increasingly being shifted from long-term treatment efforts to emergency response efforts. Between fall 2010 and spring 2016, counseling center resources devoted to "rapid access" services increased by an average of 28 percent, whereas the allocation of resources to "routine treatment" decreased by 7.6 percent.[20]

How individuals interpret these findings is often a function of how they feel about higher education in general. Some political pundits and culture warriors have pointed to anecdotes of students complaining about "microaggressions" and insisting on "trigger warnings" and "safe spaces" as evidence that colleges and universities are coddling "snowflake" students, making them more entitled and less resilient. They perceive the increase in demand for counseling services as further evidence of this trend.

Others, including most higher-education professionals, dismiss such characterizations of the problem. Rather than ridicule students for seeking help, these individuals are interested in better understanding the causes of—and solutions to—their problems. They attribute students' mental health challenges to a multitude of interrelated factors, including economic stress, the effects of drug and alcohol use, intense pressure to succeed academically, and a host of other broad societal, cultural, and personal factors.[21] They worry that failure to address the mental health crisis on college campuses has the potential to increase the use of unnecessary medications, the use of shorter and less effective forms of psychotherapy, the reliance on unprofessional self-help and peer support systems, and the number of students whose problems go untreated.

Many have noted that the college mental health crisis has seemingly emerged at the same time as social media. Many believe that social media and smartphones are exacerbating students' mental health challenges and, perhaps, causing new ones. Some worry that viewing highly "curated" lives of others on social media can lead to envy and depression and adversely affect one's happiness and self-esteem.[22] It can also lead individuals to feel that others are having rewarding experiences while they are not (e.g., fear of missing out, or FOMO).

Some observers worry that social media users have supplanted authentic relationships with virtual friendships evidenced by "likes" and "shares" but void of emotional nourishment.[23] Others have pointed out the persistent nature of social media and the psychological toll of being unable (or unwilling) to "unplug," which can result in higher stress, sleep disturbances, and depression.[24] Obsession with online media has even been likened to drug abuse and gambling addiction.[25]

Higher-education professionals have often been at a loss over what to do about these concerns. Given the popularity of sites like Facebook, Twitter, and Instagram, it is unrealistic to believe that colleges and universities are capable of preventing (and perhaps even dissuading) students from using these technologies. Thus, higher-education professionals have opted to harness the power of these very technologies to address students' mental health challenges.

Facing intense pressure from internal and external constituencies, colleges and universities have attempted to bolster their mental health services. This includes enhanced training for counselors, online confidential mental-health screening and consultation, and training for students, faculty, and staff to provide mental health support. It also involves integrating social media into marketing campaigns and informing students of third-party resources that can replace or supplement the services provided on campus.

There is no shortage of social media and smartphone applications aimed at improving users' mental health. Smartphone applications such as MoodKit, Anxiety Coach, Pacifica, and Talkspace market themselves as resources that help users foster preventative measures and coping techniques.

Other applications are based on crowdsourcing, with users helping each other with their mental health needs. An application called Koko, for example, works in conjunction with a number of sites, including Facebook, Twitter, and Tumblr. The application uses artificial intelligence to interpret users' posts and, if it detects a crisis (e.g., it interprets the person to be a threat to themselves or others), connects that individual with an appropriate service like Crisis Textline. If the application detects a mental health issue that is manageable, the post is passed along to other Koko users, who respond using a simple psychological technique called "reframing" that helps the post's author think about his or her unique challenges in a new, more optimistic way. Users are provided a brief tutorial on reframing when they sign up for the application to facilitate this peer-to-peer counseling.[26]

Rather than simply serve as a broker between students and third-party applications, some institutions are taking a more formal approach to integrating these types of technologies into their student health programs. Fifteen universities, including the University of California, Davis and Rutgers, have a contract with Just in Case, a smartphone application that offers a menu of seven simple choices, including "I'm struggling to cope," "I'm worried about a friend," and "I might hurt myself." Students are guided to appropriate resources on their campus and in their community based on their selection.[27]

There is very little research on the impact these types of social media and smartphone applications have on students' mental health. Regardless, higher-education professionals are optimistic they can alleviate some of the demand for campus mental health services by serving as a broker between students and these technologies. The key is to do so in a way that helps students develop coping skills without implying that such technologies are a substitute for professional help.

Social Media and the Wellness Challenges of At-Risk Populations

Student satisfaction has long been recognized as a predictor of student persistence.[28] Furthermore, it is an assessment outcome that is largely uninfluenced by student characteristics such as academic preparedness, educational aspirations, gender, and socioeconomic status.[29] While all students are susceptible to disappointment with their college experience, some individuals face unique challenges that social media are well equipped to mitigate.

First-Generation College Students

The transition to college can be difficult to navigate for first-generation college students. Many of them enter college feeling overwhelmed and apprehensive about their ability to succeed in and out of the classroom. These students often worry that they are behind their peers and often face anxiety about communicating with faculty and staff, which puts them at higher risk of depression, substance abuse, and dropping out. While many institutions focus on helping first-generation students with academics (e.g., writing help and remedial courses), finances (e.g., FAFSA forms and scholarships), and essential skills (e.g., time management and study practices), the social and emotional needs of these students are often ignored.

In addition to informing first-generation students of resources that can provide them with the types of academic capital enjoyed by their classmates, student affairs professionals can also help first-generation students adjust to college by reminding them that they are not alone. Social media has proven to be a successful means of communicating these messages. The annual National First-Generation College Celebration organized by the Council for Opportunity in Education and the Center for First-Generation Student Success provides a perfect opportunity to do so.

The University of Washington even built a social media tool kit for the celebration. It helped faculty, staff, and administrators communicate their support of first-generation students, highlight these students' accomplishments, and advertise the resources that are available on campus to assist those who are struggling to adapt to various aspects of the campus environment. Participants were encouraged to use the National Celebration Day hashtag #CelebrateFirstGen and the institution-specific #UWFirstGen in their social media posts.[30]

Gender, Race, Religion, and Sexuality

In addition to dealing with the typical challenges associated with transitioning to college, some student populations can be particularly susceptible to the effects of stress, anxiety, and depression that result from a combative and antagonistic political climate. There is a constant stream of xenophobia and hateful rhetoric broadcast on social media by many of the most prominent government officials and thought leaders in the country, and culture warriors routinely wage their battles on college campuses. This can leave females, racial and religious minorities, and members of the LGBTQ community, in particular, feeling alienated and exhausted.

When underrepresented students arrive at the campus counseling center, they are likely to find it not only understaffed but also lacking diversity. A recent report by the Association for University and College Counseling Center Directors found that 70 percent of the staff at the 621 college counseling centers they surveyed were white, while only 11 percent were black and 7 percent were Latinx. Furthermore, 54 percent of the centers employed no black counselors, 71 percent employed no Latinx counselors, and 98 percent employed no transgender counselors.[31] These findings highlight how important it is for student affairs professionals to help underrepresented students find supportive networks in identity-affirming spaces.

Most colleges and universities have taken steps to foster such spaces. For example, it is not uncommon for institutions to have a wide variety of underrepresented-student groups (e.g., the Black Student Association, Spectrum, and Latinx Student Alliance), and some institutions even provide a physical space for members of these groups to meet (e.g., a Black Student Union or Multicultural Center). The National Minority Mental Health Month organized by the National Alliance on Mental Illness each July gives colleges and universities an opportunity to highlight the resources and services that are available to their underrepresented students.

In addition to using the hashtag #NMMHM, each year's celebration features a unique theme with a corresponding hashtag (e.g., #NotACharacterFlaw in 2017 and #MyStoryMyWay in 2018).[32] These hashtags can give voice to underrepresented students as well as help student affairs professionals communicate their commitment to serving these students.

Of course, social media can also serve as a means of publicly shaming institutions if students feel their needs are not being met. For example, aggrieved students at the University of Iowa started a social media campaign around a hashtag, #DoesUIowaLoveMe, encouraging underrepresented students to share their stories of institutional neglect.[33] The outpouring of stories across multiple social media platforms highlighted specific problems across a wide range of campus offices and services. The university eventually responded via a tweet bearing the hashtag, stating its commitment to hearing students' concerns and improving the campus climate.[34]

International Students

Research suggests the most common challenges faced by international students are social and psychological in nature (e.g., homesickness, loneliness, depression, stress, anxiety, alienation). To assist with international students' social and cultural integration, universities help these students develop collective self-esteem and social self-efficacy. Collective self-esteem refers to an individual's self-perceived contributions of value and emotional significance to the social groups in which he or she identifies. For international students, these groups include (1) connections with friends and family in their home country, (2) people from their home country studying or living in the United States, (3) international students from other countries (particularly students from countries whose culture is similar to that of their own), and (4) U.S. citizens, including students, faculty, and staff.[35]

Social self-efficacy refers to an individual's belief that he or she is competent at creating and maintaining friendships with individuals in these groups.[36] Collective self-esteem and social self-efficacy are connected. When students believe a social group values their contributions, they are more likely to make friends with individuals in that group. Given that international students who exhibit greater levels of collective self-esteem and social self-efficacy can more effectively navigate issues that arise in and out of the classroom, universities have experimented with several means of increasing these traits.

Social media has proven to be most valuable as a means of providing international students with social support. Studies show that international students use social media to stay connected to their friends and family back home, make new friends, and develop professional relationships at the host institution.[37] This is a significant development given that in the past international students have had to bear the financial costs of communicating with friends and family in their home country, largely relying on prepaid phone cards to do so.

Universities have historically been more involved in efforts to connect to others within the host country. These efforts include connecting international students to each other by supporting various multicultural student groups on campus (e.g., Hispanic Student Association) as well as providing dedicated spaces (e.g., a multicultural center or international student union) for international students to meet each other and reflect on their unique perspective on college life. Universities can also host social gatherings that leverage logistical and academic requirements. For instance, student affairs professionals at Stanford University hosted an "I-20 signing party" where international students congregated and socialized while completing the paperwork required for a Certificate of Eligibility for Nonimmigrant Student Status.[38]

Not only do the Facebook pages created and managed by offices of international student affairs help student affairs professionals share information about logistics and academics with international students, but they also provide an online community for these students to communicate with each other. When visiting their Office of International Student Affairs' Facebook page, students can click on the "Community" tab to see posts by other people who have "liked" the page. This feature not only enables Facebook members to post content on these pages that will likely appeal to other international students but also enables international students to seek out information from their peers.

While facilitating connections with other international students is important in order to ward off depression caused by acculturation, facilitating connections with individuals from the host country is essential for international student success. Thus, student affairs professionals pursue efforts to expose international students to American culture and get them communicating with U.S. citizens. Many universities have "living and learning communities" that give international students the chance to live with American students who are pursuing the same area of study. Several institutions have also developed programs that connect individual international students to volunteer "host families."

At the University of Wisconsin at Madison, student affairs professionals have organized opportunities for international students to give presentations about their home countries at local schools and nursing homes.[39]

These efforts by student affairs professionals are intended to boost international students' collective self-esteem and hone their social self-efficacy skills.

While social media accounts created and maintained by offices of international student affairs can be a tremendous resource for connecting international students to one another, they are less adept at connecting international students to students from the host country. This is because very few American students tend to "like" (or "follow") these accounts, which is not surprising given that they are primarily used to communicate important information for international students. Nonetheless, these accounts can be an important component of strategies aimed at facilitating social interactions between these student populations by promoting offline activities and programs that bring them together.

CONCLUSION

Students can suffer from a wide range of health issues that can be detrimental to their education. These issues include common illnesses, accessibility problems, and mental health challenges such as anxiety, depression, and homesickness. The relationship between social media and student health is complex. These technologies can exacerbate existing health challenges and may even create new ones. On the other hand, social media can give voice to students who suffer from health issues, and they provide institutions with additional tools for addressing these issues. In light of this information, answering the following questions can help student affairs professionals.

DISCUSSION QUESTIONS

- Are student affairs colleagues properly trained to recognize accessibility issues related to online technologies? Are institutional resources in place to address these issues?

- How are students being encouraged to use technology in ways that facilitate self-advocacy and self-determination? What technologies are they being directed to and for what purposes?
- To what extent—and in what ways—is social media being integrated into mental health counseling routines?
- How is social media being used to address the unique needs of at-risk populations on campus?

NOTES

1. Keeling et al. 2011.
2. Farnsworth 1957.
3. Ibid.
4. Kraft 2011.
5. Madaus 2011.
6. Ibid.
7. Strom 1950.
8. Rodriguez 2011.
9. Cornell Chronicle 2018.
10. Ra et al. 2018.
11. Centers for Disease Control and Prevention 2014.
12. Khajeheian et al. 2018.
13. Gow et al. 2010.
14. West et al. 2016.
15. Lytle et al. 2017.
16. Chou et al. 2014.
17. Center for Collegiate Mental Health 2014.
18. Center for Collegiate Mental Health 2016.
19. Center for Collegiate Mental Health 2019.
20. Center for Collegiate Mental Health 2017.
21. Henriques 2014.
22. Stephens-Davidowitz 2017.
23. Brody 2017.
24. Sleek 2014.
25. Kuss and Griffiths 2012.
26. Popper 2017.
27. Easley 2013.
28. Bean 1980.
29. Astin 1991.

30. University of Washington 2019.
31. LeViness et al. 2017.
32. National Alliance on Mental Illness 2019.
33. Bauer-Wolf 2019.
34. University of Iowa 2019.
35. Crocker and Luhtanen 1990.
36. Zullig et al. 2011.
37. Li and Chen 2014.
38. Greenberg and Moore 2013.
39. Ibid.

4

SOCIAL MEDIA STRATEGIES FOR CAMPUS SAFETY

On April 16, 2007, a Virginia Tech student shot and killed two fellow students in their residence hall at 7:15 in the morning. The campus community was not informed of the killings until they received an email from university officials more than two hours later. Less than twenty minutes after that message was sent, police responded to a 911 call about a shooting in another building on campus, and within minutes officials released a second email warning that a gunman was loose on campus. Ultimately, the tragedy claimed the lives of thirty-three people, including the perpetrator, and left the country grieving and in shock.

The events of that fateful morning marked the beginning of an overhaul of campus security operations at colleges and universities around the country. Students, parents, university officials, security personnel, and politicians began taking a fresh look at campus security and emergency management. Emergency preparedness task forces were formed. Attorneys general commissioned school security evaluations. Countless recommendations were made for emergency response standards and requirements.

At the same time, social networking sites like Facebook, YouTube, and Twitter were increasingly becoming ubiquitous in the lives of millions of college students. These online technologies have become central to discussions about campus security. This chapter examines the challenges faced by student affairs professionals tasked with maintaining the security of their institution and the safety of those who come into contact with it, paying close attention to how social media can both help and hinder their work.

CAMPUS SECURITY ACTORS, INTERESTS, HAZARDS, AND CONTEXTS

Prior to the creation of the first organized and professional campus police department by Yale University in 1894, security was largely maintained by janitors, groundskeepers, and faculty members tasked with mitigating fire hazards, disposing of waste, and protecting the institution's property from animals, student pranks, and local residents.[1] By the 1920s, it was common for colleges and universities to employ retired policemen to protect college property and put an end to fraternity drinking parties. It was not until after World War II that formal, organized campus police units became commonplace. The increase in professionalism during the 1950s, evidenced by the adoption of uniforms and the creation of professional organizations, did little to prepare campus security for the riots, sit-ins, and vandalism that became common at colleges and universities during the 1960s.[2]

Broadcast television drew national attention to the increasingly frequent clashes occurring between students, police, and administrators on college campuses. As protests became larger and more violent throughout the 1960s, campus police units often had to be supported by local police and members of the National Guard. Threats to campus security were increasingly hindering universities' ability to pursue their mission. Even before the massacre of four unarmed college students by the Ohio National Guard at Kent State University on May 4, 1970, it was evident that new approaches to addressing campus security and student conduct were needed. In the decades that followed, the ranks of those responsible for maintaining campus security grew to include not only local and campus police but also faculty members, academic advisers, mental health counselors, emergency managers, residence hall staff, and even the general public.

The context in which these individuals operate has changed significantly in recent years. The ability for anyone to capture photos and record video on their smartphone and immediately share it on sites like

Facebook and Twitter have placed the interactions between students, police, and university employees under a microscope. This can help keep individuals accountable for their actions.

—ᴧᴧᴧ—

Alternatively, the viral nature of social media can also result in minor incidents embarrassing the institution or leading to more significant threats. For instance, during a protest on the campus of the University of Missouri in 2015, an assistant professor of communication named Melissa Click was recorded asking for "muscle" to remove a student journalist from a public area. The video went viral on social media, resulting in Click receiving death threats as well as more than one hundred Missouri lawmakers calling for her ouster. Click was fired shortly after the state legislature voted to exclude the University of Missouri from a statewide $55.6 million budget increase and proposed cutting $8 million from the UM system.[3]

Some, it would seem, intentionally create security issues for colleges and universities in hopes that incidents will be captured and shared on social media. For example, in 2016, a popular alt-right white supremacist named Milo Yiannopoulos worked with conservative student groups at several college campuses to coordinate a series of speaking engagements billed as "The Dangerous Faggot Tour." Under the guise of promoting and protecting free speech, Yiannopoulos used incendiary rhetoric about race, religion, and gender to provoke outrage and then shared the resulting videos that were posted online of students throwing bottles, blowing air horns, and making other attempts to interrupt his presentation.

Colleges and universities had to make a choice: ban Yiannopoulos from campus and suffer the political consequences of limiting "conservative" free speech or allow him to speak and deal with the resulting political fallout associated with facilitating hate speech contrary to the values of the institution and incurring the costs associated with providing security at the events. Either way, the free speech crises manufactured by Yiannopoulos produced content that went viral on social media, boosting his notoriety and causing grief for college administrators and security personnel who already have a host of security issues to address.[4]

Despite the institutional diversity of colleges and universities, they all share a common set of security interests. These interests include the safety of the campus community (e.g., students, faculty, staff, visitors), the continuity of the institution's basic mission processes (e.g., teaching, research), the security of the institution's critical infrastructure (e.g., its facilities and support systems), the protection of the institution's reputation and financial solvency, and the preservation of the fundamental campus culture that defines the nature of higher academia. These security interests can be threatened by naturally occurring hazards (e.g., disease or weather-related calamity), accidental hazards (e.g., electrical fire or release of hazardous substance), or intentional hazards. The latter can include nonviolent crime, such as theft and vandalism, as well as interpersonal threats and violence, anonymous threats, and acts of mass violence.

In many ways, colleges and universities are similar to towns and small cities. They contain residents and workers; libraries, office buildings, dining locations, and recreation areas; streets, parking decks, and mass transit; water, electricity, and Internet infrastructure. They must manage relationships with routine emergency response such as fire and emergency medical services as well as prepare for—and inform individuals of—the types of hazards discussed above.

Despite these similarities, there are several aspects of higher education that make college campuses different from their municipal counterparts. In addition to managing relationships between lawmakers, local residents, and emergency responders, those responsible for maintaining campus security must also contend with the demands of students, parents, and teachers. These internal and external stakeholders are motivated by a mix of intrinsic and extrinsic incentives that are rarely seen outside of higher education, creating a unique set of cultural and political dynamics on college campuses.

CAMPUS SECURITY TASKS

There are a number of basic tasks associated with decreasing vulnerabilities and increasing resilience on college campuses. They include preemptively taking steps to decrease the likelihood that certain types of hazards will occur and monitoring for threats to ensure they do not. If a threat is identified, security officials assess the risk it poses and respond accordingly, all while providing relevant information to the public as events unfold. These tasks are completed by a diverse group of stakeholders working in a fragmented, complex, and multilayered system of decision making. And the work of each of these individuals has been affected by social media.

Threat Prevention and Mitigation

Discussions about threat prevention and mitigation have historically centered on the built environment. First introduced in the 1970s, crime prevention through environmental design (CPTED) seeks to evaluate an institution's physical setting to identify the factors that affect the safety and crime quotient capability of the school with the goal of keeping students, faculty, staff, and visitors safe as they traverse campus. These factors include the types of neighborhoods, housing facilities, businesses, and streets that surround the institution. They also include an assessment of fence locations, lock types, indoor and outdoor lighting, window locations, the placement of trees and shrubs, and other aspects of the built environment. CPTED assessments inform the placement of blue-light phones and security patrols, building access protocols, and other decisions intended to mitigate vulnerabilities.[5]

The terrorist attacks on September 11, 2001, helped shift the focus of discussions about campus safety to emergency management systems and communication practices. Shortly thereafter, most colleges and universities began basing their emergency operations plans on the National Incident Management System, a template for establishing structures and processes for planning and responding to a variety of hazards, including, but not limited to, weather emergencies, civil disturbances, acts of violence, or incidences involving hazardous materials. The 2008 Higher Education Opportunity Act, passed after the massacre at Virginia Tech, required virtually every university in the United States to develop emergency planning and disclosure actions that include adopting and publishing an emergency response policy, conducting annual drills, and developing communication plans that include the use of electronic media.[6]

Some of the security measures previously pursued by colleges and universities became outdated during this period due to advances in communications technologies. Blue-light phones, which became a staple on university campuses after being introduced in 1990 by a company that sold coin-operated newsstands, became largely antiquated after the advent of cellphones. As the number of emergency calls from the blue-light phones plummeted, institutions began questioning whether or not it was worth the cost of maintaining them. Some, including the University of Colorado at Boulder and the University of Nebraska at Lincoln, removed the devices from their campus. Other institutions chose to keep blue-light phones because they contribute to a sense of safety on campus, even if they remain unused.[7]

The arrival of social media technologies complicated campus security efforts by producing a digital environment that is simultaneously occupied by the same individuals that exist in the built environment and largely out of university administrators' control. Take, for example, interpersonal threats and violence. The highest rate of stalking victimization occurs among people in their early twenties and increasingly involves individuals using social media as the primary tool to track and harass others. This type of online behavior, which can have a serious impact on students' and employees' mental health and productivity, is largely unaffected by changes to the built environment. Thus, university administrators have focused on policy changes designed to curb certain online behaviors.

Policies that address online activity may arise in a number of contexts, including general conduct, sexual misconduct, student organizations, information technology and authorized computer use policies, and policies governing colleges, departments, centers, and other subunits within the institution. These policies can be written in a way that gives student affairs professionals the authority to intervene when unacceptable behaviors occur online. Doing so in a way that still respects individuals' freedom of speech, however, is no easy task. After all, there is a generally agreed upon notion that institutions of higher learning are a marketplace of ideas where controversial speech is not only accepted but valued.

Some forms of speech, such as true threats, are not protected under the First Amendment. The courts have even upheld statutes that prohibit harassment involving less than a true threat of bodily harm when they involve conduct that a reasonable person should know would cause substantial emotional distress in others. Colleges and universities are well within their right to create policies that prohibit explicit threats against specific individuals, regardless of whether such threats are made on campus or online.

The law is more nebulous, however, when it comes to university administrators' restrictions on speech based on vague standards related to "discourteous," "offensive," or "annoying" content that can too easily be applied arbitrarily. One might argue that individuals with controversial views can take advantage of the limited scope of university policies, damaging the institution's reputation and inciting legitimate security concerns as a result. This fear explains why some students have requested physical "safe spaces" where certain ideas and forms of speech are prohibited.

Alternatively, one might view policies designed to promote civil discourse as privileges of—or oppressive tools wielded by—those with power, and therefore suspect. Policies that seemingly regulate individuals' tone of voice by way of limiting certain types of expression can be used to diminish their legitimacy and hamper their calls for activism. Many students, faculty, and staff reject these kinds of paternalistic policies.

Institutions can differ significantly in their approach to regulating online speech. In September 2013, a journalism professor at the University of Kansas posted a tweet on his personal Twitter account that read, "The blood is on the hands of the #NRA. Next time, let it be YOUR sons and daughters," in reference to an attack by a lone gunman who killed twelve people at the Washington Navy Yard in Washington, D.C. The tweet prompted outrage from conservative state lawmakers and resulted in the professor being temporarily removed from the classroom and assigned administrative duties that could be completed away from campus.

Soon thereafter, the Kansas Board of Regents passed a strict policy restricting faculty and staff at the state's six universities, nineteen community colleges, and six technical colleges from saying anything on social media that would incite violence, disclose confidential student information, or be "contrary to the best interests of the university." Critics argued that the policy was overly broad and would infringe upon academic freedom.[8]

The University of Tennessee took a very different approach after a professor at the UT College of Law tweeted a statement on his personal Twitter account in September 2013 that read, "Run them down," in reference to a large group of protesters that blocked a highway in Charlotte, North Carolina. Despite calls from many students, faculty, and alumni for the professor to be punished or fired for inciting violence, school officials refused to do so, arguing that public institutions cannot punish their employees for expressing their political beliefs on their personal social media accounts. Once school officials announced that no disciplinary actions would be pursued, the professor deleted the insensitive tweet and issued an apology.

These cases demonstrate both the need for clear policies that address employee conduct on social media and the difficulty of obtaining a consensus regarding what those policies should say.

In addition to developing policy solutions, student affairs professionals can leverage their institution's official accounts on social media to communicate the importance of emergency preparedness and offer tips on how to reduce the likelihood of various hazards.

For instance, the Department of Public Safety at Ohio State University used its Twitter page to encourage students, faculty, and staff to sign up for the institution's Buckeye Alert System, inform them of best practices for reducing the risk of house fires during winter, and introduce them to key security personnel on campus.[9] By developing clear policies and communicating action plans, colleges and universities can help individuals mitigate and prepare for a wide range of disasters.

Threat Monitoring

"If you see something, say something." The phrase, which was featured in an advertising campaign on New York City subways and buses in 2002, has become a national slogan in post-9/11 America.[10] It reflects, and perhaps contributes to, the anxiety people have about criminal behavior. As tens of millions of individuals flocked to sites like Facebook and Twitter, the call for vigilance extended to content posted to social media with the aim of pinpointing potential problems before they manifest themselves.

Such calls are not without merit. Student affairs professionals have traditionally monitored for warning signs such as excessive absences from class, complaints from fellow classmates, evidence of substance abuse, problems in residence halls, criminal offenses, and other behaviors that might require intervention. Today, troubled individuals experiencing a mental health crisis and would-be criminals sometimes lay out their plans—or at least hint at them—on popular social media sites.

In response to these trends, a number of companies emerged to provide security solutions to schools by harnessing data from social media profiles. They claim to give schools the information they need to keep their campuses safe by analyzing aggregated data from several social media platforms. The exact business model and monitoring practices of these companies is often opaque. Some companies base their service on strictly defined, campus-centered virtual barriers, called "geofences."

Others evaluate data from a broader area, including locations outside campus and specific individuals' accounts regardless of their location. The software enables the monitoring of multiple real-time feeds using a complex set of filters based on GPS coordinates, image recognition software, and keywords such as *fight*, *suicide*, *bomb*, and *gun*. The software is purportedly complex enough to differentiate between phrases like "I bombed the exam" and "I'm going to bomb the school." Some companies perform the monitoring in-house, while others merely license their software to schools to use on their own as they see fit.[11]

Despite the complexity of the software, the problem with social media monitoring is that the whole context of a post is almost never available to the individual or software reading it. Personality quirks, inside jokes, and a whole host of protected speech is likely to be lost on them.

Without that crucial context, all kinds of innocuous posts might appear threatening.

The number of "false positives" produced by monitoring systems raises a host of concerns about privacy, profiling, and the effects of creating a surveillance state on college campuses. The lack of strict legal guidelines regarding how student communications are monitored and tracked is of particular concern. Critics also point to a lack of firm metrics for measuring the effectiveness of social media monitoring services, arguing that schools are basing their purchasing decisions on the strength of a sales pitch rather than empirical evidence.[12]

Some administrators worry that social media monitoring could expose their institutions to additional liability and possible violations of the law. The high-profile murder of Jeanne Clery in her residence hall at Lehigh University in 1986 spurred Congress to pass the Jeanne Clery Disclosure of Campus Security Policy and Campus Crime Statistics Act (hereafter referred to as the Clery Act), a federal statute enforced by the U.S. Department of Education requiring all institutions of higher education that participate in the federal student financial aid program to disclose information about crime on their campuses and in the surrounding communities. Failure to report evidence of criminal activity uncovered via social media monitoring could be interpreted as a violation of the Clery Act. Furthermore, most institutions lack the resources necessary to respond to every perceived threat communicated online. Some colleges and universities have decided that the best course of action is to avoid social media monitoring altogether.[13]

Threat Identification

Correctly identifying the nature and location of threats is no easy task. Permeable boundaries between campus and community, as well as the number and types of buildings on campus, can hinder such efforts. Likewise, there are obstacles posed by the lack of dress codes, the prevalence of backpacks, and routine flows of large numbers of individuals traversing campus.

The ability of social media users to remain anonymous exacerbates the challenges of threat identification. Rather than physically confronting their victims, perpetrators can do so online. Victims of online harassment may have no idea who is responsible for the harassment. Most social media applications, including Facebook and Twitter, merely require individuals to use a valid email to open an account.

An account on one social media application can often be used to open an account on another social media application. Nothing prevents individuals from starting an account using an alias. Some social media applications have even been explicitly built around the notion of privacy. Anonymity can appeal to those who have grown tired of public posturing at the expense of honesty and authenticity. It can also appeal to those with devious actions in mind.

In 2013, two students at Furman University in South Carolina launched a social media smartphone application called Yik Yak, which allowed users to anonymously create and view discussion threads that originated within a 1.5-mile radius. Unlike other applications that allowed users to share content anonymously, Yik Yak was intended for sharing content with those in proximity to the user, making the application well suited for college campuses. Once a thread was started, other users could contribute to the stream by writing responses and "voting up" or "voting down" the post.

Yik Yak became an immediate concern for school administrators. High schools and colleges alike began routinely going on lockdown based on anonymous bomb threats and threats of gun violence communicated on the application. In addition to death threats, university officials had to grapple with harassment, hate speech, and threats of sexual violence against faculty and students communicated on Yik Yak.

Given the anonymous nature of the posts, colleges and universities were largely powerless to deal with the havoc wreaked by the application. While schools could block access to Yik Yak on their Wi-Fi networks, banning students from using the application outright would have been a violation of free speech and would not have worked anyway given that students could still use the application on their phones with their cell service. Facing intense pressure from parents, educators, and lawmakers, Yik Yak began placing restrictions on what and where posts could be made. The company introduced virtual fences that would render the application unusable on school property, though doing so proved to be difficult on sprawling university campuses.[14]

Generally speaking, Yik Yak zealously protected the identities of its users, though the company did work with authorities when evidence of specific, actionable threats emerged. Their cooperation resulted in a number of high-profile arrests. For instance, a student at Michigan State University was arrested for threatening a shooting on campus.[15] Similarly, a student at the University of Missouri was arrested for "making a terroristic threat" toward students of color, posting messages on Yik Yak that included "I'm going to stand my ground tomorrow and shoot every black person I see" and "Don't go to campus tomorrow."[16] And a Virginia Tech student was arrested for a post on Yik Yak that warned of another "4.16 moment," a reference to the April 16, 2007, shooting detailed at the beginning of this chapter.[17]

Risk Assessment

The few campus emergency manager positions that existed at the time of the Virginia Tech massacre were predominantly focused on natural disasters such as severe weather and earthquakes. Over the last decade, colleges and universities have increasingly developed specialized, proactive threat assessment teams to deal with a wide range of crises.[18] These teams consist of a variety of stakeholders, including administrators and student affairs professionals, campus security and police, mental health professionals, and institutional legal counsel. There is often membership crossover between threat assessment teams and crisis response teams (discussed below).

The purpose of the threat assessment team is to assess known threats and take early action to diffuse potentially violent situations. These teams must be mindful of the legal requirements related to retention, security, and release of student information dictated by statutes like the Family Educational Rights and Privacy Act and the Health Insurance Portability and Accountability Act given that they rely on information from a variety of sources for their analysis (e.g., health records, academic transcripts, financial aid, criminal records). Along with these types of documents, the content posted to individuals' social media accounts is often a key source of information for threat assessment teams.

When a threat to campus security is identified, reviewing the social media accounts of those involved can help threat assessment teams determine the substance and nature of an individual's expressions, such as whether the postings are "true" thoughts, impulsive inclinations, or a way to gain attention by "performing" for others who will view the posts.[19] To do so, threat assessment teams must be aware of the nuances of particular types of social media platforms as well as the characteristics of the individuals using them. The perceived nature of the medium can have significant implications on what and how individuals—particularly those who are young and immature—communicate.

In 2014, a student at the University of Georgia used Yik Yak to post an anonymous message that warned others at the school to stay away from the Zell B. Miller Learning Center "if you want to live" because "I'm coming with an AK," a reference to an AK-47 assault rifle. Campus officials put the campus on lockdown upon discovering the message. When arrested by police, who were able to determine the origin of the message with the assistance of Yik Yak, the student said that he intended the post to be funny and assumed it would only be read as a joke. After all, much of the content posted to Yik Yak consisted of jokes, memes, and snarky comments about mundane topics like the weather and nightlife on campus.

The individual did not expect anyone, including the police, to take it seriously. When an individual calls 911—an established emergency telephone number—they can hardly make the argument that they are just joking. It is conceivable, however, that someone using an application known for generating edgy content might presume that others share their perception of the network as a place where comments cannot be taken as serious or legitimate.

Crisis Response and Communication

Once a threat has been identified, the emergency operations plan (EOP) is activated by someone designated to do so (e.g., first responders, police officers). For minor emergencies, selected elements of the EOP can typically be activated without engaging institutional-level administrative officers. For more serious emergencies, the EOP usually calls for establishing an on-site incident command post led by an incident commander. Serious emergencies may also result in higher institutional authorities (e.g., president, vice president, provost, chief security officer) meeting at an emergency operations center (EOC), located at a designated spot on campus.

The work of the incident commander is tactical (i.e., using resources at his or her disposal to address the crisis), whereas the work of those in the EOC is strategic (e.g., addressing ongoing institutional issues and providing policy oversight). The incident commander is supported by a staff including but not limited to a safety officer, a victim liaisons officer, and a public information officer. Social media has affected the responsibilities of the latter in particular.

The public information officer serves as the conduit for information from the incident commander to internal and external stakeholders, including the media. This person's job is to gather and verify information as well as communicate information regarding the incident's cause, scope, and current situation. In addition to helping the incident commander respond to the *assessed* threat, the public information officer responds to individuals' *perceived* safety concerns to ensure their mental well-being.[20] The latter are often more significant than the former.

The increasing frequency of campus violence over the years has been generally proportional to enrollment increases, but awareness of such incidents has increased dramatically due to their coverage by mainstream national news outlets and on social media.[21] The disproportionate amount of news coverage these incidents receive results in exaggerated fears of campus violence.[22] Social media provide an outlet for these exaggerated fears and often facilitate real-time sharing of speculation and misinformation during a crisis. Research has demonstrated that electronic word of mouth has a higher diffusion speed and can reach a much larger group of recipients.[23]

Public information officers can mitigate this problem by providing accurate, accessible, and timely information, but their ability to do so can be restricted by law enforcement agencies, privacy concerns, legal constraints, and inefficient notification systems. This can leave students, parents, employees, and the media without immediate answers to their questions. The lack of transparency can lead individuals to perceive threats greater than those that actually exist and can undermine trust in university officials.

The massacre at Virginia Tech highlighted the types of problems that can plague an institution's emergency notification system. Their system included email alerts, updates posted to the university's website, a broadcast phone-mail system, and contacts with local radio and television stations. However, it lacked the ability to send text messages. More problematic was the fact that only the chief of the Virginia Tech Police Department and the Virginia Tech Policy Group could authorize the transmission of messages, and doing so required access codes held by only two other individuals, the associate vice president of university relations and the director of news and information. Furthermore, there were no prewritten messages. Each notification had to be written from scratch and approved by the policy group prior to transmission. These logistical hurdles help explain why the campus community was not informed of the first shooting until an email from university officials was received more than two hours later.[24]

Following the shooting at Virginia Tech, colleges and universities began to reprioritize the way they communicate emergencies, with the goal of providing more timely and accurate information. Today, integrated mass notification systems assist with this task by enabling universities to issue alerts simultaneously across multiple platforms, including text messaging, email, and social media. This redundancy helps create a sense of urgency, which may be lacking when only one mode of communication is used.[25]

Such redundancies can also help attenuate the unique drawbacks of each mode of communication. For example, text message alert systems require individuals to opt in, they are limited in the amount of information they can contain, and they are slower to transmit due to bandwidth limitations. While email can be transmitted faster and can contain more information, there is a risk messages will be sent to a spam or junk folder. Furthermore, students are often discouraged from checking their email while they are in class.

Colleges and universities can leverage their official social media accounts—where they have already built loyalty and trust with internal and external stakeholders—to mitigate these challenges during a crisis. Not only are social media sites more easily updated than other methods of communication, but they often display informative posts in an easily accessible timeline that can be helpful during and after an incident. Social media allow institutions to update information more continuously without having to issue additional formal emergency notifications through other channels, which should be reserved for major announcements. Furthermore, the social media accounts of various subunits on campus (e.g., Dining Services, Housing and Residence Life, Parking Services) can help university officials address questions related to multiple facets of the same incident. And, of course, the same techniques that are used to monitor social media for threats can also help public information officers refute rumors that may be circulating about safety risks.

CONCLUSION

Social media can cause headaches for those who bear the responsibility of maintaining campus security. But these online networks have also proven to be essential tools for fostering a culture of preparedness and managing information during and after a crisis. They also present student affairs professionals with an important series of questions that need to be asked and answered *before* the next crisis occurs.

DISCUSSION QUESTIONS

- How are emergency communications disseminated? Must individuals sign up to receive messages from campus authorities or do they receive them automatically? Can individuals opt out?
- Does the institution's emergency communications plan have safeguards and redundancies in place?
- Are there social media "hotlines" for reporting suspicious activities or criminal behavior (e.g., sexual assaults or drug use)?
- Does the university have policies that cover online/social media threats or harassment?

NOTES

1. Powell et al. 1994.
2. Fisher and Sloan 1995.
3. Landsbaum 2016.
4. Logue 2016.
5. Watson 2014.
6. LaBanc et al. 2010.
7. Jackson 2019.
8. Lomonte 2014.
9. Ohio State University Emergency Management 2019.
10. O'Haver 2016.

11. Winn 2016b.
12. Carollo 2015.
13. Winn 2016a.
14. Mahler 2015.
15. Grasha 2015.
16. Larimer 2015.
17. Moxley 2015.
18. Hollister and Scalora 2015.
19. Shaw and Westfall 2015.
20. Kaminski et al. 2010.
21. Drysdale et al. 2010.
22. Kaminski et al. 2010.
23. Kaplan and Haenlein 2011.
24. Schildkraut et al. 2016.
25. Stephens et al. 2013.

5

SOCIAL MEDIA STRATEGIES FOR CAREER AND ALUMNI SERVICES

For a significant number of students, a college degree is primarily a credential, something they need in order to move on to their chosen profession. In a recent study, over 80 percent of students cited the prospect of a job as a critical factor in their decision to enroll in college.[1] These students are highly attuned to the various ways their campus activities—both inside and outside the classroom—affect their future career success. Simply put, they want to get a good job when they graduate, and they expect their college or university to help them do so. Institutions have adjusted to this reality by providing a host of services, typically coordinated by a career center, that help students at various stages along the way to that first job.

Once students graduate, their relationship to the university changes. They are no longer considered students but rather alumni. Accompanying this transition are a host of changes regarding why and how institutions maintain contact with these individuals. This chapter explores how the services provided to students and alumni have changed in these areas and how social media has affected the manner in which both career centers and alumni organizations deliver their services.

CAREER SERVICES

College is supposed to be the pinnacle of a student's educational experiences. Having completed their degree requirements, students are supposed to be ready to join the workforce. In the past, colleges and universities tended to be populated by upper-class individuals who often had a family network to rely on when it came to job prospects. They frequently knew where they were going to be employed long before graduation. As collegiate education became more widespread, the number of individuals who did not enjoy these types of social connections multiplied. As a result, colleges and universities began providing career services intended to assist students who did not have jobs already waiting for them after graduation.

As soon as students step foot on campus, there are things the career center can do to help them prepare for the job market. For example, students who are unsure of what major to choose or what types of careers correspond to certain majors are often guided to the career center, where they are provided with personality tests, job outlooks/forecasting, and career coaching. Career centers can provide direction to students who, if nothing else, can use help translating their interests and aptitudes into majors and eventually into jobs.

Once students have chosen a major, career centers can help them move on to the preparation phase of their career development where they build job-hunting skills. Career centers can provide students assistance in writing résumés, administering mock interviews, and hosting etiquette dinners. These are documents and skills that students will need to be successful once job-hunting begins in earnest, and their importance cannot be overstated. A false step in any of these areas can mean the difference between getting a job and getting a rejection letter.

After students have selected their majors, taken their courses, and honed their job-hunting credentials and skills, they are ready to go on the job search. Fortunately, they do not have to do it alone. In this final phase, the job-hunting phase, career centers once again provide a variety of services to students. They routinely host job fairs and on-campus recruiters, while also providing links to internships and other networking opportunities with employers.

Career centers have the capacity to assist students from beginning to end of the career development process. Unfortunately, these centers are often not used to their fullest capacity due to a variety of challenges faced by students and the career services professionals who serve them. Social media can help colleges and universities better prepare their students for life after graduation by providing new means of addressing many of them.

There are a number of challenges associated with delivering career services, some of which might not be obvious. Many young people spend their entire lives thinking of higher education as an end rather than a means to an end. From a rather young age, they are implored to think about how their grades and extracurricular activities will affect the likelihood they will be admitted to certain types of colleges and the likelihood they will receive scholarships to attend them. Once students arrive on campus, it can take time for them to reconceive college not as an end in itself but rather as a means to a career. It is not surprising that many students do not even know their campus has a career center, let alone what services it offers.[2]

Even once students are made aware of the services provided by the career center, it may prove difficult to get them to take advantage of these services. Two-thirds of career centers in a recent survey reported difficulties engaging students.[3] Some students may be more difficult to engage than others. On more affluent campuses, for example, there may be reduced use of career services since students in the upper socioeconomic strata may already have built-in job-hunting networks.[4]

On other campuses, it can be a challenge to engage first-generation college students, minority students, transfer students, and nontraditional students. These underrepresented groups of students often feel like the services offered by career centers are largely focused on people in other groups and will therefore not be applicable to them.[5] This is a shame since the services offered by most career centers are applicable to all students. In fact, research suggests that career services can positively affect the job prospects of minority students in particular.[6]

Career services need to be offered in a way that students find useful. A recent Gallup survey of college graduates indicated that over half, about 52 percent, visited career services at some point in their college career. About 17 percent found their contact with career services to be "very helpful," while an equal number reported that it was "not helpful at all."[7]

One career services professional noted that some students arrived thinking that career services was going to do all the work and just place them in a job. Another offered the following take: "One of the challenges is helping students understand that going to the career office is a multioccasion, multiyear experience, not just going 'at least once.' Sometimes students think they'll go one time for thirty minutes to get everything they need, but it's not that simple."[8] And this phenomenon is not uncommon. Forty-four percent of career centers surveyed in 2019 indicated that they also struggled with unrealistic student expectations.[9]

Other challenges are not unique to career services. Career services professionals report being overworked and understaffed. There is never enough time, people, or resources to handle demand.[10] In recent years, a focus on creating "career-ready" students has resulted in individual professors or academic programs incorporating career services materials into their courses or program requirements. This trend has expanded the footprint of career services, but it has increased workload as well.

SOCIAL MEDIA AND CAREER SERVICES

For many career service centers on university campuses, the lure of social media was powerful. It was one more tool that could be used to encourage students to come to the career center and discover the services it offered. Many centers jumped on the social media bandwagon with little thought given to any systematic planning or how these new platforms would fit into existing communications strategies.[11]

Growth has been significant, yet fitful. While a 2009 survey of career centers portrayed social media as a potentially "disturbing" phenomenon (i.e., upsetting the status quo of service offerings and delivery), a similar survey conducted a mere four years later in 2013 showed that social media use was widespread among career centers on campus. Over 95 percent of respondents used social media in one form or another. Over two-thirds of the career centers surveyed experienced moderate or significant growth in the use of social media.[12] Students have been receptive to the increased use of technology. In a 2014 survey, 85 percent of students surveyed said that it was helpful to have career-related social media services.[13]

This increased use and popularity of social media did not necessarily translate into considerably more staff time spent on social media. Just under half of the respondents in the 2013 survey reported spending roughly one to five hours each week working on the unit's social media. Less than 15 percent spent ten or more hours each week.[14] It appears that social media use is broad but not deep.

Three platforms are most consistently used by career services professionals. Surveys show that Facebook is used by over 90 percent of responding career centers. Most career centers have a Facebook page where they share information about upcoming events, workshops, and other educational material. These are open groups anyone can join or follow. Twitter and LinkedIn followed closely behind Facebook in terms of popularity.[15] Of the three, LinkedIn was the only social media platform ranked as "highly effective" by career services professionals.[16]

Social media is becoming increasingly important in all three stages of a student's journey through career services: selecting a major, building skills, and the job search itself. By providing meaningful opportunities for students and strengthening their relationship with career services professionals, these tools have resulted in new approaches to tackling old problems at each stage. Many of the third-party social media tools students can use in various stages of the job search are available for free. In many instances, the job of the career services professional is to link students with the appropriate social media tools at the appropriate time. By helping students use these tools effectively, career services professionals can achieve their ultimate goal: a job for the student.

Selecting a Major

Many students feel considerable pressure to arrive on campus having already selected an academic major. They think that they should know what it is they want to study and how that will lead them to a career. They worry that getting their choice "wrong" will lead to wasted time and money in college and an unsatisfying career. They often feel that their choice at this stage is an irrevocable one. This attitude, in turn, ratchets up the pressure even more.

It is not uncommon for students to think that they are unique in their indecisiveness. The reality is that a significant number of students arrive on campus with no major. Some have narrowed it down to a degree ("I think I like sciences."), while others are truly undecided. Even those who have chosen a major often find themselves switching majors. Though the rates varied per major, one recent study indicated that about one-third of all students change their major while in college. Almost 10 percent change majors more than once.[17] This is clearly an area where students could use the assistance of career services.

While most of the information career services professionals historically shared with students was in the form of printed material, career services offices also eventually began to incorporate CAGS (computer-assisted career guidance systems) into their arsenal. Many of these CAGS featured online chats, career-oriented videos, and virtual calendars. These computer-based services served as the precursors to many of the social media tools currently used by career services today. They were used to help students match their skill sets to a major and then to a career.

One thing that social media can do at this stage is to help break down traditional barriers typically faced by students contemplating these decisions. The thought of visiting a faculty member or any career services professional in that person's office on campus can be intimidating for many students, especially when they would have to admit that they are undecided about what they want to do. They do not want to be embarrassed in this way.

Social media allows for students to do this exploration in the privacy of their own space. Career services websites can offer the aptitude quizzes and assessment rubrics, allowing students to do them at their own pace and follow up with professionals when they feel comfortable. This can help some students move from the "I'm really clueless about this" phase to the "I'm ready to talk to someone about this" phase.

The structure found at Marquette University's Career Service Center is fairly typical.[18] It has an "exploration" section with self-assessments and career assessments. It includes the commonly used Myers-Briggs exercise, which is designed to help inform students about their strengths and preferences. There is also a link to My Next Move, an online tool that allows students to explore a variety of careers. CareerExplorer by Sokanu is another such tool with links to over 800 careers and over 140 personality traits.

There are also other ways that students can use social media to help choose a major. One way is to select a leader in a particular career field and follow that person on social media. For instance, if a student is interested in computers, that individual might follow Bill Gates of Microsoft or Tim Cook of Apple. Another way is to identify commonly used hashtags related to specific careers (e.g., #studentaffairs, #SApro, and #SAchat) and then follow discussions consisting of posts bearing those hashtags. Students can also join a variety of groups with a particular career focus on LinkedIn or other social networks.[19] They can just "lurk," seeing what others have to say and offer in these online communities, or they can become active participants from the relative safety of their computer. These low-cost, low-pressure ways of exploring a major or career path help reduce traditional socioeconomic or physical barriers to access.

Building Skills

Social media is also increasingly used in the second phase, where students develop documents and skills in preparation for the job search. As noted earlier, many students think they can just visit the career center once or twice and walk out with a perfect résumé and impeccable interview skills. They often do not appreciate the time and effort that should go into creating effective job-search documents and skills.

The reality is that a well-crafted résumé takes time and precision. The same can be said for interviews. These are often awkward and stressful interactions with important outcomes hinging on one's performance. Effective job-hunting skills, like any other skill set, are honed by time and practice. Career services professionals have the capacity to assist students in this area and the expertise to know what skills are needed and how to sharpen them. Increasingly, social media has become key to these efforts.

Students need to know how to craft a well-organized résumé, be sure they are wearing proper professional attire, demonstrate appropriate meal etiquette, and possess professional interviewing habits. Social media can help develop all these skills and more. Online, interactive workshops can build writing skills. Instagram and YouTube have shown to be good vehicles for assisting students with making sure they are appropriately dressed and exercising proper etiquette.

For instance, Brown University's CareerLAB (LAB stands for life after Brown) web page sports a calendar, an e-newsletter, student stories, and a blog. One additional area this university uses quite well is YouTube. The CareerLAB's YouTube channel offers videos on a host of things: interviews, information sessions, tips and tricks, alumni stories, and even a game show–style information video.[20]

Networking and Job Searching

Once students have selected a major, completed their degree coursework, and developed those job-searching skills, they are ready to begin the final stage: networking and job searching. This is perhaps the most daunting stage, one that can seem overwhelming to many students. Career services can mitigate some of this stress. Princeton University career services has a Facebook page that also conveys information to students but, perhaps most strikingly, is filled with pictures and videos of students. The message is clear: these are the types of people we help—and they look just like you.[21]

Career services offer a variety of tools to assist students at this stage. Princeton's career services Twitter account has over six thousand followers. Each Monday it, in conjunction with other universities, posts job opportunities for students and alumni using the hashtag #MondayOpenings. There are videos that depict students discussing various aspects of their internship/jobs and how the career center helped them obtain those positions. There is also a calendar and a newsfeed on the university's website that is updated regularly to make students aware of events and services.

Surveys also show that many career centers employ "how-to" tips on social media; offer advice from experts; conduct contests, polls, and surveys; maintain blogs with information on job market trends; and interview students and staff.[22] For instance, one career center offered "Myth-Busting Mondays" and "Re-Tweet Tuesdays." Another advertised "Ask-an-Expert" days on its LinkedIn platform.[23]

Neumann University, a small Catholic liberal arts college, recently ran similar campaigns. One event called Knight-2-Knight was a dinner that paired a student with an alum who worked in the student's field of interest. A second program, Notes from a Knight, featured handwritten notes from alumni to prospective admitted students welcoming them into the Neumann family. Both instances use social media to bring students and alumni together in more personal, intimate ways.[24]

There are even times when social media bring career services and alumni services together. DePaul University's "HireDePaulBlog" is an important component of their ASK (Alumni Sharing Knowledge) Program, a program designed to connect alumni with current DePaul students who share an interest in a common field of employment.[25] Similarly, Macalester University's career and alumni services work together with social media outreach including webinars and their Exploreship program, which matches undergraduates with nearby alumni.[26]

The University of Pennsylvania also makes extensive use of social media technology in its career services center, Penn and Beyond. Its web page houses an extensive blog that is full of reports from students about the important role career services played in their successful internship or job hunt. There are also video podcasts for smartphones, Vimeo videos, and a 38,000-strong alumni network on LinkedIn. The web page also has an interactive bot that allows page visitors to use this chat feature to direct them to the information or services they need.[27]

It is not just Ivy League schools that make extensive use of social media in career services. Bryant, a small private university in the northeast, also uses social media on its career services web page. There is a section on the web page called Success Stories where students share their experiences with career services. Bryant also has a feature where they use Portfolium to allow students to create digital portfolios that they can use for internships and job hunting. These portfolios can contain images, papers, videos, and other digital content that students and job hunters can employ to "fill out" their résumés.[28] In short, career services centers are now using social media in a wide variety of ways. While a few platforms, such as Facebook, Twitter, and LinkedIn, dominate the landscape, colleges are being increasingly innovative in the ways they use technology to reach students.

SOCIAL MEDIA CHALLENGES

Even though virtually all college and university career centers have some type of social media presence, a variety of challenges remain. Many of these challenges were completely predictable. In some instances, they were exacerbated by career centers who jumped into the social media pool without clear plans or objectives. It is not uncommon for institutions to address these challenges as they arise, often in an ad-hoc, piecemeal fashion.

One of the most fundamental issues that is frequently mentioned is the lack of support for social media use from higher-ranking college administrative officials. More precisely, career services providers do not usually encounter opposition to their social media use, but there is not any overt support for it either.[29] This administrative ambivalence can be a positive in one sense because it gives career centers the opportunity to experiment with a variety of social media approaches, using those that work and discarding those that do not. On the other hand, this ambivalence often translates into other problems—lack of resources, lack of clear policies, and a sense that there is no real campus leadership on social media issues.

This administrative ambivalence can also be tied to the frequent lack of social media planning in the area of career services. Over half of the career centers who use social media do so without any formal strategy. There is a general sense that social media can accomplish (or supplement old tools to help accomplish) a variety of goals, yet this is rarely put together in any comprehensive framework.[30] How does one know whether the effort put into social media is successful?

Some career centers do have formal goals and metrics they use to measure their success when it comes to social media usage (although over a third have none whatsoever). One of the more popular metrics is to simply use the dashboard analytics associated with the various platforms.[31] One can count the number of tweets or Facebook posts or blog entries. It is also possible to count the number of people who "follow" or "like" a page/account/post. Many social media platforms also allow users to ascertain how many people their account is reaching (e.g., "traffic" numbers). These analytics provide some empirical measure of how many people are exposed to a center's social media messages and in some cases how well received those messages are.

While they do not provide in-depth information, these types of analytics can tell how many people have looked at a given picture, video, or post. In many instances, one can also tell who looked and when. User demographics are sometimes available too. This provides some basic information to career services organizations about who is actually receiving their messages. This is particularly useful in an era in which all college units are increasingly being asked to empirically justify their budgets.

The most widespread concern raised in virtually all surveys about social media is privacy and the ethical issues associated with it.[32] Two-thirds of the respondents in one survey went as far as to describe privacy issues as a moderate-to-significant barrier in the expanded use of social media.[33] Social media platforms like Facebook and Twitter blur the line between personal and professional. Students often prefer to keep their personal and professional lives separate, reserving social media for friends and close acquaintants.

And what are the ethical obligations if career services professionals see examples of unethical or illegal behavior on student social media? Career services centers who use social media would be wise to develop policies that, as clearly as possible, delineate the personal and professional boundaries and expectations so that both students and career services personnel know where the lines are.

Perhaps one of the most ironic challenges to the use of social media by career centers is its sometimes-limited impact. While social media can provide an additional conduit for getting information to students, one of the defining characteristics of social media is that they are designed to be interactive forums. However, over three-quarters of those career services professionals surveyed indicated that social media only had a slight impact on the level of student engagement.[34] It takes time and effort to maintain social media platforms, and if they are only reaching a small number of people or simply replicating the impact of other information-sharing mechanisms, career centers should assess whether the pursuit of a quality social media presence is the best use of time and resources.

Some colleges have devoted funds to social media–related positions. Macalester College created a special technology and operations coordinator position. This person deals solely with the Career Development Center's social media accounts on Facebook, Twitter, Instagram, LinkedIn, and Pinterest.[35] These types of positions are still not very common. Social media responsibilities are more frequently tacked onto employees' other responsibilities or given to student workers who are assumed to be adept at social media (which may or may not be true). Training largely consists of isolated workshops or quite simply on-the-job training.[36] As a result, the quality of social media efforts on campus can be rather haphazard.

It is fair to say that most college and university career services centers have added social media to the repertoire of tools they use to deliver their services to students. Many campus centers have been quite creative in the different ways they use technology. The one common theme among all these approaches is that social media allows colleges to put the student at the center of the message in a way that was much more difficult to accomplish in earlier decades. Video testimonials, blogs, and pictures bring these student stories to life and help to make career services somewhat more personal than they were before the widespread use of social media.

Career services professionals who use social media point to a variety of advantages it brings. At a very basic level, it increases the visibility of career services and creates the capacity to provide more information to students on an almost instantaneous basis. More people are aware of what they have to offer students. It also helps increase attendance at career center events. Social media also increases the level of communication between career services professionals and students. In a recent survey, many career services directors indicated that using social media—being up on the latest technology—increased their credibility with students and other colleagues.[37] Others point out that social media can be a cost-cutting tool. It is free, and sharing information via social media platforms can be infinitely cheaper than printed materials—which can become quickly outdated—or purchasing advertising time on radio or television.[38]

Social media use by campus student affairs units does not end when students get a job and leave campus. It simply enters a different phase. Alumni services is also beginning to see how social media can be leveraged to help it accomplish its goals with the university's graduates. Social media does not just help students get a job; it helps them remain in contact with the university after they leave.

ALUMNI SERVICES

The term *alumnus* is most frequently used to describe a person who has graduated from a school, usually a college or a university. Almost all colleges and universities have some type of alumni services on campus. They help keep students in touch with their alma mater and provide a variety of amenities. Like other aspects of the campus experience, alumni services have also made increasing use of social media platforms to help them accomplish their goals.

—∞∞—

It was not long after colleges and universities appeared in the United States that alumni groups began to form. In 1792, Yale College alumni began an organization based on class structure (e.g., the Class of '92) that eventually sent out newsletters to keep graduates informed of events at the college. This organization quickly grew, founding local chapters of Yale graduates. It also began to solicit donations for the university.

Alumni groups began to form in other universities too.[39] The alumni group from Williams College formed in 1821, while the University of Virginia alumni association formed in 1838. Princeton's was founded in 1826. Princeton's alumni group undertook the ambitious goal of raising $100,000 for the college, and although it only reached half that goal, the effort foreshadowed the thousands of alumni fund-raising campaigns that would follow.[40]

Alumni services at colleges and universities today provide an incredible variety of amenities. Many—in conjunction with career services—offer job hunting and networking services. Most offer a lifetime email address or access to credit cards, travel deals, and bargains on everything from magazines to health insurance. They market university merchandise, sponsor university alumni awards, and hold reunions. Others hold homecoming events, maintain alumni databases, and encourage alumni to mentor current students.

The key for alumni services through all these efforts is communication. By keeping in touch with alumni, colleges and universities can use the items noted above to keep them returning to campus and invested in the mission of the institution. This is important for building relationships with alumni that can result in them contributing their time, their talents, and perhaps most importantly, their money.[41]

ALUMNI SERVICES AND SOCIAL MEDIA

Alumni services, like other departments on campus, deliver services and information using the means at their disposal. In the 1980s, this meant printed materials supplemented by television, radio, or videotapes.[42] In the 1990s, these materials were supplemented with static websites and email. The advent of Web 2.0 technologies added social media to these means of communication. As technology has changed, so too have the communication strategies used by university offices.

Communication and Connection

As multichannel communication has become the new normal, the key challenge for alumni services has been to find the best mix of channels for a particular audience. Different demographics may prefer to receive information in different ways. One 2012 study that examined how millennials preferred to be contacted by nonprofit agencies revealed distinct preferences for electronic communication. Sixty-five percent wanted to be directed to a website. Just over half wanted to interact via some type of social media. Just under half expressed a preference for e-newsletters, while only 18 percent favored print materials and even fewer wanted face-to-face contact.[43] One might expect the preferred communications mix to be different for other demographic groups, such as baby boomers.

One of the key takeaways from this is that younger alumni are more desirous of electronic communications. As a result, there has been a proliferation of social media pages and platforms employed by alumni services departments across the country. Research has shown that social media networks can provide low-cost networks and strengthen community, help build social capital, and reach larger audiences with greater frequency—all goals that alumni services seek as they attempt to retain the connection between students and their alma mater.[44] Research also shows that social media overtures are most effective when they supplement existing networks.[45] They provide alumni services with additional channels to communicate with their target population and help diversify and multiply the university's messages.

While it has become clear that social media can enhance an alumni center's messaging, it remains a challenge to effectively implement social media programs due to staffing issues. The vast majority of alumni organizations do not employ a full-time social media person. Research also shows that buy-in from the college or university president is also an important component of making social media work. About 40 percent of presidents are on some form of social media,[46] and their presence signals that the entire university—right up to the top—is committed to using social media effectively.

A recent study showed that 79 percent of those holding a college degree also had a Facebook account.[47] This is where the alumni are, and it is why 80 percent of alumni centers in a 2015 survey confirmed that they advertised on Facebook to help achieve their goals: expanding their reach, raising awareness, and fund raising.[48] Size does not appear to matter. Over two-thirds of community college alumni centers use Facebook to communicate with alumni,[49] as do large flagship universities such as the University of Michigan's alumni association, a group with almost six hundred thousand alumni.[50]

The University of Michigan's alumni association Facebook page is in many ways typical. It is very visual—there are lots of pictures and videos. Topics include sports, stories about Ann Arbor, university history, alumni profiles, and current student activities. Pages like this are usually fairly active, with daily posts.[51] This approach is also consistent with research that shows that posts with pictures and videos are shared and liked far more frequently than those with only text.[52]

The use of social media to share stories is a common theme among university alumni pages. The University of Oxford's page encourages alumni to share stories about trips they have taken or events they have attended. It also ran a campaign titled #ThreeLittleWords, which asked alumni to post pictures of themselves describing Oxford, or their time at Oxford, in three words.[53] These types of campaigns are designed to ignite a sense of nostalgia, which is key to keeping alumni invested in the institution.

Facebook also has more direct ways of inducing action from its members. Pages can contain a variety of "calls to action," such as allowing users to click on links that allow alumni to update their information for alumni services, make reservations for an upcoming event, or donate to the university. One can also set up polls on Facebook. This builds in a "curiosity loop." People not only answer the polls; they log on later to see the results. Facebook also allows for "tagging," or identifying people in photos, and this can be set up in a way so that anyone who views the photo has the capacity to tag individuals in the picture. This too spreads the reach of the alumni services Facebook page.[54]

Twitter is also widely used by alumni services. Twitter, in the words of one researcher, can create a buzz, capture events as they unfold, and make users feel like they were there.[55] Alumni associations regularly "live-tweet" events such as homecoming, reunions, or other on- and off-campus events. Alumni services also use Instagram and YouTube to provide visual depictions of their services, alumni stories, campus events, and a variety of other things. These social media overtures are often used to drive traffic to the university's web page, where initial messages can be reinforced and additional information can be provided.

Raising Money

One of the most important—and most challenging—aspects of alumni services is the task of raising money to support the university and its endeavors. As noted earlier in the chapter, university alumni associations have been in the business of raising money since the nineteenth century. One recent survey indicated that roughly a quarter of all private donations made to colleges and universities were received from alumni.[56] While most alumni will not begin donating large sums of money to the institution immediately upon graduation, student affairs professionals can use this time to establish contact with them and begin building a relationship that might yield future contributions.

Social media has become a vital tool for accomplishing these tasks. It is important to remember, however, that social media are not taking the place of traditional fund-raising campaigns but rather supplementing them in a targeted way. In fact, most institutions (including community colleges) are now finding that it is crucial to have both traditional and online components to their fund-raising plans.[57]

One of the most important factors in fund raising for universities is finding a way to maintain a connection with alumni. Research has shown that social media platforms can help cultivate and maintain relationships among students, staff, and alumni.[58] It also has demonstrated that in some instances social media marketing can be as good as or even better than traditional marketing campaigns.[59] More to the point, there are also studies that have shown a direct correlation between social media usage and charitable giving and/or volunteering behaviors.[60]

Younger alumni in particular are on social media already in exceptionally high numbers, and they, unlike their more senior counterparts, are used to being contacted electronically. Some prefer to give online as opposed to more traditional methods. For them, it is simple, quick, and easy. And some of these online donors are people who historically have not responded to traditional fund-raising campaigns.[61]

CONCLUSION

Both career services and alumni services are increasingly making use of social media on college campuses. Social media are not just another means for spreading information; they have proven to be an indispensable tool for putting both current and former students in the middle of the picture in a way that was not truly possible before. This is particularly true when it comes to assisting students in the job search process and keeping them in contact with the university after they graduate. The questions below can assist units who want to make more extensive use of these online technologies.

DISCUSSION QUESTIONS

- How does social media fit into career and alumni services' communication routines? How is social media being used to supplement or replace traditional forms of communication (e.g., pamphlets, phone calls, face-to-face gatherings)?
- In what ways are social media being used to connect students with alumni in their career field? Is this being accomplished at different stages of a student's career (e.g., recruitment, selection of major, job search preparation)?
- Are social media networks being used to gather job placement and job satisfaction information? How is this information being used by career and alumni services as well as other campus units?
- How are student affairs colleagues using social media to keep alumni connected and invested in the university?
- How do the demographic and giving patterns of the institution's alumni lend themselves to integrating social media into fund-raising campaigns?

NOTES

1. Fadulu 2016.
2. Ibid.
3. GMAC 2019.
4. Fadulu 2016.
5. Gallup 2016.
6. Ibid.
7. Ibid.
8. New 2016.

9. GMAC 2019.
10. Ibid.
11. Kubu 2012.
12. NACE 2013; Kubu 2014.
13. Gaul 2014.
14. Kubu 2014.
15. NACE 2013; Kubu 2012.
16. NACE 2013.
17. Lederman 2017.
18. Marquette University 2019.
19. Anselmo 2012.
20. Brown University 2018.
21. Princeton University 2018.
22. Kubu 2012.
23. Ibid.
24. Neumann University 2018.
25. DePaul 2018.
26. DiMaria 2012.
27. University of Pennsylvania 2018.
28. Bryant University 2018.
29. NACE 2013.
30. Kubu 2014.
31. Ibid.
32. Osborn et al. 2014.
33. NACE 2013.
34. Kubu 2014.
35. DiMaria 2012.
36. Kubu 2014.
37. Osborn and LoFrisco 2012.
38. Sampson and Osborn 2014; NACE 2013.
39. Foreman 1989.
40. Ibid.
41. Ibid.
42. Webb 1989.
43. Northfell et al. 2016.
44. Ellison et al. 2007.
45. boyd and Ellison 2007.
46. Ponisciak n.d.
47. Advancement Form 2017.
48. Ponisciak n.d.
49. Hall 2016.

50. University of Michigan Alumni Association 2019.
51. Ibid.
52. Advancement Form 2017.
53. University of Oxford 2018.
54. Advancement Form 2017.
55. Litsa 2017.
56. Farrow and Yuan 2011.
57. Martin 2013; Mudrick et al. 2016; Skari 2014.
58. Bahfen and Wake 2015.
59. Icha and Edwin 2016.
60. Farrow and Yuan 2011.
61. Kowalik 2011.

CONCLUSION

The purpose of this book is to help higher-education professionals better understand how social media affects the various facets of student affairs, including admissions and enrollment, academic services, student health and well-being, campus security, and career and alumni services. It summarizes the development of these areas and examines how social media can exacerbate or mitigate the key challenges associated with them. The questions at the end of each chapter are intended to help individuals think about how to apply the concepts and examples to their own institutions. To conclude, we encourage individuals to be savvy, social, scrupulous, strategic, and supportive as they embark on their own social media initiatives.

BE SAVVY

The savvy higher-education professional is well informed, experienced, and astute. Everyone who works in higher education, and student affairs in particular, has a responsibility to be informed about current issues in higher education. This includes matters related to social media. It is important to be knowledgeable about the role of technology in students' lives and the potential impacts it might have on their physical, mental, and academic well-being.

Student affairs professionals need to understand the basic characteristics of social media and have a working knowledge of how various platforms facilitate communication and interaction. Finding examples of how these technologies have been used by student affairs professionals to further individual and institutional goals is tremendously helpful. Finally, it is important to understand the context in which discussions and uses of online technologies take place. An awareness of the legal, ethical, and political implications of social media use on college campuses can help individuals avoid costly mistakes.

The stories that appear in the *Chronicle of Higher Education* can help individuals stay abreast of broad trends and timely issues that are important to colleges and universities. It can also be beneficial to follow the social media accounts of relevant organizations, such as the National Association of Colleges and Employers, the National Academic Advising Association, and the American Association of Collegiate Registrars and Admissions Officers. For content specifically addressing issues related to technology, sites like EdTechMagazine.com and CampusTechnology.com provide more specialized content.

This may seem like an absurd amount of information to gather and track given individuals' other responsibilities. Fortunately, there are online tools that can do much of the work. For example, Hootsuite and Tweetdeck can help curate social media posts based on hashtags and specified search parameters. An initial investment of time spent setting up these tools to properly curate posts from across multiple social media sites can save individuals a tremendous amount of time in the long run.

Perhaps the best way to learn about social media is to simply start using them. Experiment with new and existing social media to better understand the technologies students use and to imagine how they might be used to achieve institutional goals. Consider experimenting using a personal account or anonymous "dummy account." This will prevent leaving a trail of abandoned institutional accounts on social media platforms that proved to be a poor fit. If experimentation proves useful, invest the time and resources necessary to have a properly branded institutional account on the platform.

BE SOCIAL

The social higher-education professional is connected and engaged. It is important for individuals working in higher education to recognize that they are not alone. There are thousands of student affairs professionals around the world, and it has never been easier for them to connect with one another. LinkedIn and Twitter, in particular, are excellent resources for professional networking. The latter allows individuals to follow others' accounts as well as add them to "lists." Not only can individuals create their own lists, but they can follow lists created by other users. This allows them to search for lists of student affairs professionals, particularly those who work in their specific area, or create a list of such individuals if none already exist.

On Twitter, higher-education professionals should consider following and using relevant hashtags like #EdTech, #EduTech, #HigherEdTech, and #eLearning, among others. To better understand how technologies are being used specifically in the realm of student affairs, individuals should follow and use #SApro (for those working in student affairs) and #Sagrad (for graduate students). Likewise, they should participate in #Sachat, where there are structured and regularly scheduled live chats about student affairs in higher education. Again, a tremendous amount of time can be saved by using tools like Hootsuite and Tweetdeck to aggregate posts bearing these hashtags and keep track of likes, comments, and new followers.

Finally, individuals should seek out and work with technophiles on their own campus. It is not uncommon for those with an interest in technology to form working groups. These types of collaborative endeavors give individuals an opportunity to meet and discuss new tactics and strategies for using social media on campus.

BE STRATEGIC

The strategic higher-education professional is intentional and opportunistic. Individuals should consider their objectives, think about how they can be advanced by using social media, and make sure they choose the right tool for the job. Facebook's features make it ideal for scheduling and advertising events, whereas Twitter might be better suited for real-time question-and-answer sessions.

Remember, these tools can be used together. If an office decides to host a live question-and-answer session on Twitter, they can create an event page on Facebook for it, which allows other users to indicate whether they are "interested" or "going." Once the chat goes live, a photo of staff gathered to respond to the questions can be posted to Instagram with a caption encouraging individuals to participate in the chat by using the relevant hashtag on Twitter.

A social media post that does not facilitate an action is typically a wasted opportunity. When posting to social media, individuals should make sure the post enables other users to take the action necessary to complete the objective. If an institution posts about its recent placement on a "Top Ten Colleges for Outdoor Enthusiasts" list in an effort to attract prospective students but does not include a link to the application portal, its post has failed to facilitate the objective.

It is important for individuals to work with their colleagues across campus to coordinate social media activities. Cross-posting material from smaller units on campus across more popular accounts can help promote activities. It can also increase awareness of institutional resources and guide individuals to the units best suited to address their needs.

It can also be helpful to leverage external programs and conversations. For example, individuals should consider how to take advantage of "awareness months" (e.g., National Minority Mental Health Month) to promote campus resources (e.g., the counseling center or multicultural center) by posting to social media using the designated hashtags (e.g., #NMMHM). By actively participating in online conversations on social media, individuals can achieve multiple goals at once, such as raising their profile among prospective students while simultaneously advertising resources to current students.

BE SCRUPULOUS

The scrupulous higher-education professional is principled and diligent. The work of student affairs professionals is essential to the mission of colleges and universities. It is important that they do their job well in order to serve the interests of the institution and address the needs of various constituents, including students and their parents, alumni, employees, and the public. They should think about how the content they post to social media will be perceived by diverse populations and constituencies and how those perceptions might affect the institution.

When individuals engage in online conversations about sensitive or contentious issues, they need to anticipate the types of responses they might encounter. They should ensure that they have the capacity to monitor their social media accounts. Likewise, they need to have a comment policy in place and abide by it. Even when university employees engage in such conversations on their personal accounts, they need to be cognizant of university policies that address employee behavior.

Finally, individuals need to be aware of the political context in which they operate as well as the legal and ethical obligations they have to students. Higher-education professionals need to understand how their social media efforts might be affected by the Health Insurance Portability and Accountability Act, the Family Educational Rights and Privacy Act, the Clery Act, and the Americans with Disabilities Act. Sadly, individuals must also consider how their efforts might be "weaponized" by those who wish to score cheap points in political culture wars. The last thing individuals want is for their social media initiatives to go from being an asset to a liability.

BE SUPPORTIVE

The supportive higher-education professional contributes to a strong Internet technology culture on campus. This may involve working with individuals or units who lag behind the technological curve to get them up to speed using social media. Informing them of the types of issues raised in this book and helping them become savvier, social, scrupulous, and strategic using the tips laid out above is a starting point.

Broader efforts to support social media use on campus can also strengthen institutions' Internet technology culture. Those tasked with the responsibility of managing others should establish clear expectations and policies regarding the ways that subordinates manage institutional social media accounts. They should also incentivize subordinates' social media efforts and provide them with proper training. If individuals are having trouble getting others on campus to participate in their social media initiatives, it may help to produce tool kits with prepackaged content such as logos, hashtags, photographs and videos, and links to relevant university websites.

BE SUCCESSFUL

Higher-education professionals who exhibit the traits outlined above stand a much better chance of being successful when it comes to incorporating social media into their professional lives. The key is to think systematically and act intentionally. Define what success looks like (i.e., set goals), understand how to achieve it (i.e., identify objectives), and then observe whether or not the objectives are advancing the goals (i.e., collect and analyze data). Social media has opened up a whole new world of communications, one that can make colleges and universities even better places to grow and learn. There may be growing pains, but the benefits will ultimately be worth the costs.

BIBLIOGRAPHY

Advancement Form. 2017. "Best Practices for Engaging Your Alumni on Facebook." Located at: https://www.advancementform.com/resources/best-practices-engaging-alumni-facebook/. Last accessed: 2 July 2019.

Alemán, Ana Martinez, and Katherine Lynk Wartman. 2009. *Online Social Networking on Campus: Understanding What Matters in Student Culture*. New York: Routledge.

Allen, Matthew. 2012. "An Education in Facebook." *Digital Culture & Education* 4(3): 213–25.

American College Personnel Association. 1949. *Student Personnel Point of View*. Washington, DC.

———. 1937. *Student Personnel Point of View*. Washington, DC.

Anselmo, Kevin. 2012. "Using Social Media to Choose a College Major." Located at: http://experientialcommunications.com/using-social-media-to-choose-a-college-major/. Last accessed: 4 July 2019.

Appalachian State University. 2019. Located at: https://www.facebook.com/search/top/?q=Appalachian%20state%20top%20five%20suggestions. Last accessed: 26 July 2019.

Astin, Alexander W. 1991. *Assessment for Excellence: The Philosophy and Practice of Assessment and Evaluation in Higher Education*. New York: Macmillan.

———. 1975. *Preventing Students from Dropping Out*. San Francisco: Jossey-Bass.

Atkinson, Richard C., and Saul Geiser. 2015. "The Big Problem with the New SAT." *New York Times*, 5 May, A23.

Bahfen, Nasya, and Alex Wake. 2015. "Tweeting, Friending, Reporting: Social Media Users Among Journalism Academics, Students and Graduates in the Asia-Pacific." *Pacific Journalism Review* 21(1): 173–84.

Baier, John L. 1994. "Assessing and Enhancing Technological Competencies of Staff." In *Technology in Student Affairs: Issues, Applications, and Trends*, edited by John L. Baier and Thomas S. Strong. Lanham, MD: University Press of America.

Baier, John L., and Thomas S. Strong, eds. 1994. *Technology in Student Affairs: Issues, Applications, and Trends*. Lanham, MD: University Press of America.

Bauer-Wolf, Jeremy. 2019. "#DoesUIowaLoveMe." *Inside Higher Ed*, 27 February. Located at: https://www.insidehighered.com/news/2019/02/27/u-iowa-students-launch-digital-campaign-around-minority-issues-campus. Last accessed: 1 July 2019.

Baxter Magolda, Marcia. 2001. *Making Their Own Way: Narratives for Transforming Higher Education to Promote Self-development*. Sterling, VA: Stylus.

Bean, John. 1980. "Dropouts and Turnover: The Synthesis and a Test of a Causal Model of Student Attrition." *Research in Higher Education* 12: 155–87.

Bethel School District v. Fraser 478 U.S. 675 (1986).

Boucher, Jason. 2014. "How UNH Used Social Media to Welcome New Wildcats During Summer Orientation & Move-In Weekend." 22 September. Located at: http://www.edsocialmedia.com/2014/09/how-unh-used-social-media-to-welcome-new-wildcats/. Last accessed: 14 May 2019.

Bowen, William, Matthew Chingos, and Michael McPherson. 2009. *Crossing the Finish Line: Completing College at America's Public Universities*. Princeton, NJ: Princeton University Press.

boyd, danah m., and Nicole Ellison. 2007. "Social Network Sites: Definition, History, and Scholarship." *Journal of Computer-Mediated Communication* 13(1): 210–30.

Brody, Jane E. 2017. "Hooked on Our Smartphones." *International New York Times*, 9 January. Located at: https://www.nytimes.com/2017/01/09/well/live/hooked-on-our-smartphones.html. Last accessed: 1 July 2019.

Brown, Paul G. 2016a. "College Student Development in Digital Spaces." *New Directions for Student Services* 155(62): 59–73.

———. 2016b. *College Students, Social Media, Digital Identities, and the Digitized Self* (Doctoral dissertation). Boston College, Chestnut Hill, MA.

Brown University CareerLAB. 2018. Located at: https://www.brown.edu/campus-life/support/careerlab/. Last accessed: 4 July 2019.

Bryant University Amica Center for Career Education. 2018. Available at: https://career.bryant.edu/. Last accessed: 4 July 2019.

Buckingham, David. 2008. *Youth, Identity, and Digital Media*. Cambridge, MA: MIT Press.

Burnett, Darlene J. 2002. "Innovation in Student Services: Best Practices and Process Innovation Models and Trends." In *Innovation in Students Services: Planning for Models Blending High Touch/High Tech*, edited by Darlene Burnet and Diana Oblinger. Ann Arbor, MI: Society for College and University Planning.

Cabellon, Edmund T., and Reynol Junco. 2015. "The Digital Age of Student Affairs." *New Directions for Student Services* 151(Fall): 49–61.

"Campus Overload—Facebookgate, the 2010 Edition." 2010. *Washington Post* (February) Available at: http://voices.washingtonpost.com/campus-overload/2010/02/_admissions_officers_a_bit.html. Last accessed: 7 July 2018.

Carollo, Malena. 2015. The Secretive Industry of Social Media Monitoring." *Christian Science Monitor*, 16 November. Located at: http://projects.csmonitor.com/socialmonitoring. Last accessed: 27 July 2019.

Carter, Rebekah. 2018. "7 Alumni Engagement Best Practices for Universities." Sprout Social, 26 March. Located at: https://sproutsocial.com/insights/alumni-engagement-best-practices/. Last accessed: 4 July 2019.

Center for Collegiate Mental Health. 2019. *2018 Annual Report*. Publication No. STA 19-180.

Center for Collegiate Mental Health. 2017. *2016 Annual Report*, Publication No. STA 17-74.

Center for Collegiate Mental Health. 2016. *2015 Annual Report*, Publication No. STA 15-108.

Center for Collegiate Mental Health. 2015. *2014 Annual Report*, Publication No. STA 15-30.

Centers for Disease Control and Prevention. 2014. *Trends in Prevalence of Obesity, Dietary Behaviors, and Weight Control Practices: National YRBS: 1991–2013*. Located at: https://www.cdc.gov/healthyyouth/data/yrbs/index.htm. Last accessed: 4 July 2019.

Chou, Wen-ying Sylvia, Abby Prestin, and Stephen Kunath. 2014. "Obesity in Social Media: A Mixed Methods Analysis." *Translational Behavioral Medicine* 4(3): 314–23.

Clinedinst, Melissa, and Anna-Maria Koranteng. 2017. "2017 State of College Admission." *National Association for College Admission Counseling*. Located at: https://www.nacacnet.org/globalassets/documents/publications/research/soca17final.pdf. Last accessed: 4 July 2019.

College Student Educators International (ACPA) & Student Affairs Professional in Higher Education (NASPA). 2015. *Professional Competency Areas for Student Affairs Educators*. Located at: https://www.naspa.org/images/uploads/main/ACPA_NASPA_Professional_Competencies_FINAL.pdf. Last accessed: 4 July 2019.

Colorado State University. 2019. "Office of Admissions (Playlist)." Located at: https://www.youtube.com/watch?v=MkavQH9HYiY&list=PLB1DAAE3061528ABE. Last accessed: 4 July 2019.

Constantinides, Efthymios, and Marc C. Zinck Stagno. 2011. "Potential of the Social Media as Instruments of Higher Education Marketing: A Segmentation Study." *Journal of Marketing for Higher Education* 21(1): 7–24.

Cornell Chronicle. 2018. "Cornell Launches New Disability Awareness Campaign." Located at: https://news.cornell.edu/stories/2018/02/cornell-launches-new-disability-awareness-campaign. Last accessed: 4 July 2019.

Crocker, Jennifer, and Rita Luhtanen. 1990. "Collective Self-esteem and Ingroup Bias." *Journal of Personality and Social Psychology* 58: 60–67.

Crookston, Burns B. 1994. "A Developmental View of Academic Advising as Teaching." *National Academic Advising Association Journal* 14(2): 5–9.

———. 1972. "A Developmental View of Academic Advising as Teaching." *Journal of College Student Personnel* 13: 12–17.

Curmudgucation. 2017. Located at: http://curmudgucation.blogspot.com/2017/07/did-sat-unmask-grade-inflation.html. Last accessed: 24 July 2019.

Cuseo, Joe. n.d. *Academic Advisement and Student Retention: Empirical Connections & Systemic Interventions*. Located at: https://www.uwc.edu/sites/default/files/imce-uploads/employees/academic-resources/esfy/_files/academic_advisement_and_student_retention.pdf. Last accessed: 4 July 2019.

Daily Trojan. 2015. *USC Cribs*. Located at: https://www.youtube.com/watch?v=6d9pbyIabCE&list=PLzJ5G-QqnQWGmEgdiXSO_6VNDu1kiBZ5P. Last accessed: 4 July 2019.

Dartmouth College. 2014. *Live Admissions Q&A on Facebook*. Located at: https://news.dartmouth.edu/events/event?event=31932#.XFyd91VKi70. Last accessed: 5 July 2019.

DePaul University. 2018. *Alumni Sharing Knowledge*. Located at: https://resources.depaul.edu/alumni-sharing-knowledge/Pages/default.aspx. Last accessed: 5 July 2019.

DiMaria, Frank. 2012. "Alumni, Social Media and Internship Help Graduates Find Jobs." *The Hispanic Outlook in Higher Education; Paramus* 22(13): 28–30.

Drysdale, Diana A., Modzeleski, William, and Simons, Andre B. 2010. *Campus Attacks: Targeted Violence Affecting Institutions of Higher Education*. U.S. Secret Service, U.S. Department of Homeland Security, Office of Safe and Drug-Free Schools, U.S. Department of Education, and Federal Bureau of Investigation, U.S. Department of Justice. Washington, D.C., 2010. Located at: https://www2.ed.gov/admins/lead/safety/campus-attacks.pdf. Last accessed: 7 August 2019.

Dupere, Katy. 2017. "This Social Media Challenge Lifts Up Black Students with Financial Support and Mentorship." *Mashable*, 13 June. Located at: https://mashable.com/2017/06/13/itavchallenge-black-college-students/#Vmir9VHDE5qf. Last accessed: 5 July 2019.

Dwyer, John Orr. 1989. "A Historical Look at the Freshman Year Experience." In *The Freshman Year Experience*, edited by M. Lee Upcraft et al. San Francisco: Jossey-Bass.

Easley, Julia Ann. 2013. "New UC Davis Website Turns Smartphones into Lifelines for At-Risk Students." Located at: https://www.ucdavis.edu/news/new-uc-davis-website-turns-smartphones-lifelines-risk-students/. Last accessed: 5 July 2019.

Elling, Theodore W., and Stuart J. Brown. 2001. "Advancing Technology and Student Affairs Practice." In *The Professional Student Affairs Administrator*, edited by Roger Winston et al. New York: Brunner-Routledge.

Ellison, Nicole, Charles Steinfield, and Cliff Lampe. 2007. "The Benefits of Facebook 'Friends': Social Capital and College Students' Use of Online Social Network Sites." *Journal of Computer-Mediated Communication* 12(4): 1143–68.

Ensher, Ellen A., Suzanne C. de Janasz, and Christian Heun. 2004. "E-mentoring: Virtual Relationships and Real Benefits." Paper presented at the Academy of Management Annual Meeting, New Orleans, LA.

Erikson, Erik H. 1968. *Identity: Youth and Crisis*. New York: W.W. Norton & Company.

Fadulu, Lola. 2018. "Why Aren't College Students Using Career Services?" *The Atlantic*, 20 January. Located at: https://www.theatlantic.com/education/archive/2018/01/why-arent-college-students-using-career-services/551051/. Last accessed: 5 July 2019.

Farkas, Karen. 2014. "Colleges Find New Ways to Recruit Today's Social Media Savvy High School Students." *Cleveland.com*, 6 April. Located at: https://www.cleveland.com/metro/index.ssf/2014/04/colleges_find_new_ways_to_reac.html. Last accessed: 5 July 2019.

Farnsworth, Dana L. 1957. *Mental Health in College and University*. Cambridge, MA: Harvard University Press.

Farrow, Harmonie, and Y. Connie Yuan. 2011. "Building Stronger Ties with Alumni Through Facebook to Increase Volunteerism and Charitable Giving." *Journal of Computer-Mediated Communication* 16: 445–64.

Fisher, Bonnie S., and John J. Sloan III. 1995. *Campus Crime: Legal, Social and Policy Perspectives*. Springfield, IL: Charles C. Thomas.

Forman, Robert. 1989. "Alumni Relations—A Perspective." In *Handbook for Alumni Administration*, edited by Charles H. Webb. New York: Macmillan.

Gallagher, Phillip J., and George E. Demos, eds. 1983. *Handbook of Counseling in Higher Education*. New York: Praeger.

Gallup, Inc. and Purdue University. 2016. *Great Jobs. Great Lives. The Value of Career Services, Inclusive Experiences and Mentorship for College Graduates*.

Gaul, Patty. 2014. "Many College Career Centers Don't Get a Passing Grade." *T+D* 68(6): 24.

Georgetown Stories. n.d. Located at: https://www.youtube.com/channel/UC56ylmPGjs9hDfUZvhOA_Qw. Last accessed: 5 July 2019.

Georgetown University. n.d. "Admitted Students: Online Chats." Located at: https://admittedstudents.georgetown.edu/online-chats. Last accessed: 5 July 2019.

Gillispie, Brian. 2003. "History of Academic Advising." Located at: http://www.nacada.ksu.edu/Resources/Clearinghouse/View-Articles/History-of-academic-advising.aspx. Last accessed: 5 July 2019.

Gordon, Virginia N. 2006. *Career Advising: An Academic Advisor's Guide*. San Francisco: Jossey-Bass.

———. 1994. "Developmental Advising: The Elusive Ideal." *NACADA Journal* 14(2): 71–75.

———. 1992. *Handbook of Academic Advising*. Westport, CT: Greenwood Press.

———. 1984. *The Undecided College Student: An Academic and Career Advising Challenge*. Springfield, IL: Charles C. Thomas.

Gow, Rachel W., Sara E. Trace, and Suzanne E. Mazzeo. 2010. "Preventing Weight Gain in First Year College Students: An Online Intervention to Prevent the 'Freshman Fifteen.'" *Eating Behaviors* 11(1): 33–39.

Graduate Management Admission Council (GMAC). 2003. "Tackling the Top 10 Challenges in Career Services." *Graduate Management News*, September–October. Located at: https://www.gmac.com/why-gmac/gmac-news/gmnews/2003/september-october/tackling-the-top-10-challanges-in-career-services. Last accessed: 5 July 2019.

Grasha, Kevin. 2015. "Former MSU Student Sentenced for Yik Yak Shooting Threat." *Lansing State Journal*, 4 March. Located at: https://www.lansingstatejournal.com/story/news/local/2015/03/04/yik-yak-sentence/24373391/. Last accessed: 5 July 2019.

Greenberg, Ashley, and Sarah Moore. 2013. "Supporting International Students Across Student Affairs." Custom research brief for the Education Advisory Board. Located at: http://saa.gatech.edu/sites/default/files/documents/custom/supporting_international_students_across_student_affairs1.pdf. Last accessed: 5 July 2019.

Grubb, Kevin, Shannon Conklin, and Megan Wolleben. 2016. *Career Counselor's Guides to Social Media in the Job Search*. Located at: http://www.naceweb.org/career-development/best-practices/the-career-counselors-guide-to-social-media/. Last accessed: 16 August 2018.

Hanover Research. 2014. *Trends in Higher Education Marketing, Recruitment, and Technology*. Located at: https://www.hanoverresearch.com/media/Trends-in-Higher-Education-Marketing-Recruitment-and-Technology-2.pdf. Last accessed: 5 July 2019.

BIBLIOGRAPHY

Harrington, Christine, and Theresa Orosz. 2018. *Why the First-Year Seminar Matters: Helping Students Choose and Stay on a Career Path.* New York: Rowman & Littlefield.

Hazelwood School District v. Kuhlmeier 484 U.S. 260 (1988).

Henriques, Gregg. 2014. "What Is Causing the College Student Mental Health Crisis?" *Psychology Today.* Located at: https://www.psychologytoday.com/us/blog/theory-knowledge/201402/what-is-causing-the-college-student-mental-health-crisis. Last accessed: 5 July 2019.

Higher Education Marketing. 2013. *Consistent Website Experiences with Intuitive Navigation.* Located at: http://www.higher-education-marketing.com/blog/intuitive-navigation. Last accessed: 5 July 2019.

Hirt, Joan B. 2006. *Where You Work Matters: Student Affairs Administration at Different Types of Institutions.* Tuscaloosa: University of Alabama Press.

Holbrook, Margaret W. 1981. *An Analysis of Policies and Programs for Increasing Student Retention in Institutions of Higher Education in Georgia.* Dissertation Abstracts International 42(10A): 4322.

Hollister, Brandon A., and Mario Scalora. 2015. "Broadening Campus Threat Assessment Beyond Mass Shootings." Faculty Publications, Department of Psychology. Located at: http://digitalcommons.unl.edu/psychfacpub/816. Last accessed: 27 July 2019.

Hoover, Eric. 2010. "Application Inflation: When Is Enough Enough?" *New York Times,* 7 November, ED, 20.

Huesca, Robert. 2013. "How Facebook Can Ruin Study Abroad." *Chronicle of Higher Education* 59 (14 January). Located at: https://www.chronicle.com/article/How-Facebook-Can-Ruin-Study/136633. Last accessed: 5 July 2019.

Hurwitz, Michael, and Jason Lee. 2018. "Grade Inflation and the Role of Standardized Testing." In *Measuring Success,* edited by Jack Buckley, Lynn Letukas, and Ben Wildavsky. Baltimore, MD: Johns Hopkins University Press.

Icha, Omoyza, and Agwu Edwin. 2016. "Effectiveness of Social Media Networks as a Strategic Tool for Organizational Marketing Management." *Journal of Internet Banking & Commerce* 21(S2): 1–19.

Indiana University. 2016. *#IUsaidYes,* 29 September. Located at: https://youtu.be/5TcIbksAXoo. Last accessed: 5 July 2019.

Indiana University of Pennsylvania. Office of Housing, Residential Living, and Dining. 2019. Located at: www.facebook.com/iupohrld/. Last accessed: 5 July 2019.

Indiana University–Purdue University at Indianapolis Study Abroad, 2015. Facebook Page. Located at: https://www.facebook.com/photo.php?fbid=963096633712807&set=o.1662589 3679&type=3&theater. Last accessed: 5 July 2019.

Inside Higher Ed and Gallup. 2017. *2017 Survey of College and University Admissions Directors.* Located at: https://www.insidehighered.com/booklet/2017-survey-college-and-university-admissions-directors. Last accessed: 5 July 2019.

Institute of International Education. 2017. "International Student Enrollment Trends, 1948/49-2016/17." *Open Doors Report on International Educational Exchange.* Located at: http://www.iie.org/opendoors. Last accessed: 5 July 2019.

International Student Services, Texas A&M University. 2013. Facebook Page. Located at: https://www.facebook.com/events/541951322506461/. Last accessed: 5 July 2019.

International Student Services, University of Wisconsin–Madison. 2019. Facebook Page. Located at: https://www.facebook.com/pg/ISSatUW/events/?ref=page_internal. Last accessed: 5 July 2019.

Jackson, Lily. 2019. "Emergency Blue-Light Phones Are a Symbol of Safety. Is Symbolism Worth Thousands?" *The Chronicle of Higher Education,* 25 January. Located at: https://www.chronicle.com/article/Emergency-Blue-Light-Phones/245552. Last accessed: 5 July 2019.

Jaggars, Shanna Smith, and Melinda Mechur Karp. 2016. "Transforming the Community College Student Experience Through Comprehensive, Technology-Mediated Advising." *New Directions for Community Colleges* 2016(176): 53–62.

Jaschik, Scott. 2017. "The Freshman Who Lied Her Way In." Located at: https://www.insidehighered.com/admissions/article/2017/08/28/u-rochester-revokes-admissions-offer-student-who-lied-her-way. Last accessed: 7 August 2019.

Jaschik, Scott, and Doug Lederman, eds. 2017. "2017 Survey of College and University Presidents: A Study by *Inside Higher Ed* and Gallup."

Jenkins, Greg, Kenneth Lyons, Ruth Bridgstock, and Lauren Carr. 2012. "Like Our Page—Using Facebook to Support First Year Students in Their Transition to Higher Education. A Practice Report." *The International Journal of the First Year in Higher Education* 3: 65–72.

Johnson, Jenna. 2011. "Westminster Class of 2015 Bonds via Facebook Photos." Located at: https://www.washingtonpost.com/blogs/campus-overload/post/westminster_class_of_2015_bonds_via_facebook_photos/2011/04/19/AF4vb2CE_blog.html?utm_term=.b7cb618b4321. Last accessed: 6 July 2019.

Junco, Reynol. 2014. *Engaging Students Through Social Media: Evidence-Based Practices for Use in Student Affairs*. San Francisco: Jossey-Bass.

Kaminski, Robert J., Barbara A. Koons-Witt, Norma Stewart Thompson, and Douglas Weiss. 2010. "The Impacts of the Virginia Tech and Northern Illinois University Shootings on Fear of Crime on Campus." *Journal of Criminal Justice* 38(1): 88–98.

Kaplan, Andreas, and Michael Haenlein. 2011. "Two Hearts in Three-quarter Time: How to Waltz the Social Media/Viral Marketing Dance." *Business Horizons* 54: 253–63.

Kaplan Test Prep. 2017. *College Admissions Officers Say Social Media Increasingly Affects Applicants' Chances*, 10 February. Located at: http://press.kaptest.com/press-releases/kaplan-test-prep-survey-college-admissions-officers-say-social-media-increasingly-affects-applicants-chances. Last accessed: 6 July 2019.

Keefe v. Adams 840 F.3d 523 (8th Cir., 2016).

Keeling, Richard P., Trey Avery, Jennifer S. M. Dickson, and Edward G. Whipple. 2011. "Student Health." In *Rentz's Student Affairs Practice in Higher Education* (4th ed.), edited by Naijian Zhang & Associates. Springfield, IL: Charles C. Thomas.

Ketunen, Jaana, James P. Sampson Jr., and Raimo Vourinen. 2015. "Career Practitioners' Conceptions of Competency for Social Media in Career Services." *British Journal of Guidance & Counselling* 43(1): 43–56.

Khajeheian, Datis, Amir Mohammad Colabi, Nordiana Binti Ahmad Kharman Shah, Che Wan Jasimah Bt Wan Mohamed Radzi, and Hashem Salarzadeh Jenatabadi. 2018. "Effect of Social Media on Child Obesity: Application of Structural Equation Modeling with the Taguchi Method." *International Journal of Environmental Research and Public Health* 15(7): 1343–65.

Knapp, John R., and Stuart A. Karabenick. 1988. "Incidence of Formal and Informal Academic Help-seeking in Higher Education." *Journal of College Student Development* 29: 223–27.

Komives, Susan R., and Dudley Woodward Jr. 1996. *Student Services: A Handbook for the Profession*. San Francisco: Jossey-Bass.

Kowalik, Eric. 2011. "Engaging Alumni and Prospective Students Through Social Media." In *Higher Education Administration with Social Media*, edited by Laura Wankel and Charles Wankel. Bradford, UK: Emerald.

Kraft, David P. 2011. "One Hundred Years of College Mental Health." *Journal of American College Health* 59(6): 477–81.

Kruger, Kevin, ed. 2005. *Technology in Student Affairs: Supporting Student Learning and Services*. San Francisco: Jossey-Bass.

Kubu, Evangeline. 2014. "Nationwide Career Center Social Media Survey 2013: Findings and Best Practices." Paper presented at the National Association of Colleges and Employers Conference.

———. 2012. "Career Center Social Media Implementation and Best Practices: Findings of a Nationwide Survey." *NACE Journal* 72(April): 33–39.

Kuffner, Joe. 2016. "Great Social Media Idea: Life-Sized Letters." Located at: http://socialmediaforcolleges.com/blog/2016/7/19/life-sized-letters?rq=orientation. Last accessed: 6 July 2019.

———. 2013. "Great Facebook Idea: Orientation Road Signs." Located at: http://socialmediaforcolleges.com/blog/2013/4/6/great-facebook-idea-orientation-road-signs. Last accessed: 6 July 2019.

Kuss, Daria J., and Mark D. Griffiths. 2012. "Internet and Gaming Addiction: A Systematic Literature Review of Neuroimaging Studies." *Brain Science* 3: 347–74.

LaBanc, Brandi Hephner, Thomas L. Krepel, Barbara J. Johnson, and Linda V. Herrmann. 2010. "Managing the Whirlwind: Planning for and Responding to a Campus in Crisis." In *Enough Is Enough*, edited by Brian O. Hemphill and Brandi Hephner LaBanc. Sterling, VA: Stylus.

Landsbaum, Claire. 2016. "University of Missouri Professor Who Called for 'Some Muscle' During Protests Fired." *New York Magazine*. Located at: http://nymag.com/intelligencer/2016/02/university-of-missouris-melissa-click-fired.html. Last accessed: 27 July 2019.

Larimer, Sarah. 2015. "University of Missouri Police Arrest Suspect in Social Media Death Threats." *Washington Post*, 11 November. Located at: https://www.washingtonpost.com/news/grade-point/wp/2015/11/11/university-of-missouri-police-arrest-suspect-in-social-media-death-threats/?utm_term=.d704a793e29d. Last accessed: 6 July 2019.

Lavrusik, Vadim. 2009. "10 Ways Universities Are Engaging Alumni Using Social Media." *Mashable*. Located at: https://mashable.com/2009/07/23/alumni-social-media/#e6pK5tMJ2aqj. Last accessed: 6 July 2019.

Lederman, Doug. 2017. "Who Changes Majors?" *Inside Higher Ed*, 8 December. Located at: https://www.insidehighered.com/news/2017/12/08/nearly-third-students-change-major-within-three-years-math-majors-most. Last accessed: 6 July 2019.

Levin, Mary, and Joel Levin. 1991. "A Critical Examination of Academic Retention Programs for At-Risk Minority College Students." *Journal of College Student Development* 32: 323–34.

LeViness, Peter, Carolyn Bershad, and Kim Gorman. 2017. *The Association for University and College Counseling Center Directors Annual Survey*. Located at: https://www.aucccd.org/assets/documents/Governance/2017%20aucccd%20survey-public-apr26.pdf. Last accessed: 6 July 2019.

Li, Xiaoqian, and Wenhong Chen. 2014. "Facebook or Renren? A Comparative Study of Social Networking Site Use and Social Capital Among Chinese International Students in the United States." *Computers in Human Behavior* 35: 116–23.

Litsa, Tereza. 2017. "Creative Ways for Alumni Relations Teams to Use Facebook and Twitter." Located at: https://www.advancementform.com/resources/best-practices-engaging-alumni-facebook/. Last accessed: 6 July 2019.

Logue, Josh. 2016. "The Next Ann Coulter." *Inside Higher Ed*. Located at: https://www.insidehighered.com/news/2016/02/19/student-protests-and-university-cancellations-follow-milo-yiannopoulos-speaking-tour. Last accessed: 27 July 2019.

Lomonte, Frank D. 2014. "Tweet Police." *Inside Higher Ed*. Located at: https://slate.com/human-interest/2014/01/kansas-board-of-regents-social-media-policy-imperils-academic-freedom.html. Last accessed: 27 July 2019.

Long, Dallas. 2012. "The Foundations of Student Affairs: A Guide to the Profession." In *Environments for Student Growth and Development: Librarians and Student Affairs in Collaboration*, edited by Lisa J. Hinchliffe and Melissa A. Wong. Chicago: Association of College & Research Libraries.

Loyola Marymount University. 2019. Located at: https://www.facebook.com/pg/lmula/photos/?tab=album&album_id=10152488835231085. Last accessed: 7 July 2019.

Lytle, Leslie, Melissa N. Laska, Jennifer A. Linde, Stacey G. Moe, Marilyn S. Nanney, Peter J. Hannan, and Darin J. Erickson. 2017. "Weight-Gain Reduction Among 2-Year College Students: The CHOICES ACT." *American Journal of Preventive Medicine* 52(2): 183–91.

Lytle, Ryan. 2011. "5 New Ways Colleges Are Reaching High School Students." *U.S. News & World Report*, 17 October. Located at: https://www.usnews.com/education/best-colleges/articles/2011/10/17/5-new-ways-colleges-are-reaching-high-school-students. Last accessed: 7 July 2019.

Madaus, Joseph W. 2011. "The History of Disability Services in Higher Education." *New Directions for Higher Education* (June): 5–15.

Madge, Clare, Julia Meek, Jane Wellens, and Tristram Hooley. 2009. "Facebook, Social Integration and Informal Learning at University: It Is More for Socialising and Talking to Friends About Work than for Actually Doing Work." *Learning, Media and Technology* 34(2): 141–55.

Magellan Promotions. n.d. *Integrating Social Media Into Campus Tours.* Located at: http://magellanpromotions.com. Last accessed: 7 August 2019.

Mahler, Jonathan. 2015. "Who Spewed That Abuse? Anonymous Yik-Yak App Isn't Telling." *New York Times*, 9 March. Located at: https://www.nytimes.com/2015/03/09/technology/popular-yik-yak-app-confers-anonymity-and-delivers-abuse.html?module=inline. Last accessed: 6 July 2019.

Marist College. 2019. Pinterest. Located at: https://www.pinterest.com/marist/fun-dorm-ideas/. Last accessed: 7 August 2019.

Marquette University Career Services Center. 2019. Located at: https://www.marquette.edu/career-services/. Last accessed: 7 July 2019.

Martin, Hugh J. 2013. "The Economics of Word of Mouth: Designing Effective Social Media Marketing for Magazines." *Journal of Magazine & New Media Research* 14(2): 1–12.

McBride, John. 2017. "Study Abroad Programs Highlighted in Popular Instagram Takeover Series." *BYU News*. Located at: http://news.byu.edu/news/study-abroad-programs-highlighted-popular-instagram-takeover-series. Last accessed: 7 July 2019.

McClellan, George S., and Jeremy Stringer, eds. 2016. *The Handbook of Student Affairs Administration.* San Francisco: Jossey-Bass.

Miller, Steven J. 1994. "Career Planning and Placement Programs." In *Technology in Student Affairs: Issues, Applications, and Trends*, edited by John L. Baier and Thomas S. Strong. Lanham, MD: University Press of America.

Mills, Don B. 1990. "The Technological Transformation of Student Services." In *New Futures for Student Affairs: Building a Vision for Professional Leadership and Practice*, edited by Margaret J. Barr and M. Lee Upcraft. San Francisco: Jossey-Bass.

Moody, Josh. 2018. "Universities, Colleges Where Students Are Eager to Enroll." *U.S. News & World Report*, 14 January. Located at: https://www.usnews.com/education/best-colleges/articles/2018-01-23/universities-colleges-where-students-are-eager-to-enroll. Last accessed: 7 July 2019.

Morehouse University. 2019. Located at: https://www.facebook.com/events/119435724914299/. Last accessed: 7 July 2019.

Moxley, Tonia. 2015. "Yik Yak Case: Former Virginia Tech Student Pleads Guilty." *Roanoke Times*, 2 October. Located at: https://www.roanoke.com/news/crime/montgomery_county/yik-yak-case-former-virginia-tech-student-pleads-guilty/article_45a9ed23-b16a-5db0-8d9f-6e0022d9f1ae.html. Last accessed: 7 July 2019.

Mudrick, Michael, Michael Miller, and David Atkin. 2016. "The Influence of Social Media on Fan Reactionary Behaviors." *Telematics and Informatics* 33: 896–903.

National Alliance on Mental Illness. 2019. "Learn About Minority Mental Health Month." Located at: https://www.nami.org/Get-Involved/Awareness-Events/Minority-Mental-Health-Awareness-Month/Learn-About-Minority-Mental-Health-Month. Last accessed: 7 July 2019.

National Association for College Admission Counseling. 2015. *Admission Trends Survey.* Located at: https://www.nacacnet.org/globalassets/documents/publications/research/soca_chapter2.pdf. Last accessed: 7 July 2019.

National Association of Colleges and Employers (NACE). 2018. *2017–18 Career Services Benchmark Survey Report for Colleges and Universities Executive Summary.* Bethlehem, PA: NACE.

———. 2013. *Career Services Use of Social Media Technologies* (June). Bethlehem, PA: NACE.

National Center for Education Statistics. 2012. *Fast Facts—Enrollment.* Located at: https://nces.ed.gov/fastfacts/display.asp?id=98. Last accessed: 7 July 2019.

National Resource Center for First-Year Experience and Students in Transition. 2019. Located at: http://sc.edu/fye/index.html. Last accessed: 7 July 2019.

Neumann University Alumni Association. 2018. Located at: https://www.facebook.com/neumannalumni/. Last accessed: 7 July 2019.

New, Jake. 2016. "Only 17 Percent of Recent Graduates Say Career Centers Are 'Very Helpful.'" *Inside Higher Ed*, December 13. Located at: https://www.insidehighered.com/news/2016/12/13/only-17-percent-recent-graduates-say-career-centers-are-very-helpful. Last accessed: 7 July 2019.

Noel, Lee et al. 1985. *Increasing Student Retention*. San Francisco: Jossey-Bass.

Noel-Levitz, Ruffalo. 2017. *2017 E-expectations Report*. Located at: http://learn.ruffalonl.com/WEB2017E-ExpectationsReport_LandingPage.html. Last accessed: 7 July 2019.

Northfell, Amanda, Leslie Edgar, Donna Graham, and K. Jill Rucker. 2016. "Millennial Alumni Perceptions of Communications: A Look at One Land Grant University's Media Use." *Journal of Applied Communications* 100(3): 32–43.

Nuss, Elizabeth M. 2003. "The Development of Student Affairs." In *Student Services: A Handbook for the Profession*, edited by Susan R. Komives. San Francisco: Jossey-Bass.

O'Banion, Terry U., ed. 2020. *Academic Advising in the Community College*. New York: Rowman & Littlefield.

O'Haver, Hanson. 2016. "How 'If You See Something, Say Something' Became Our National Motto." *Washington Post*, 23 September. Located at: https://www.washingtonpost.com/posteverything/wp/2016/09/23/how-if-you-see-something-say-something-became-our-national-motto/?utm_term=.fea032ed3d64. Last accessed: 9 July 2019.

Ohio State University Emergency Management. 2019. Located at: https://twitter.com/OSU_EMFP. Last accessed: 9 July 2019.

Okerson, Justine R. 2016. *Beyond the Campus Tour: College Choice and the Campus Visit*. Located at: http://publish.wm.edu/cgi/viewcontent.cgi?article=1004&context=etd. Last accessed: 9 July 2019.

Osborn, Debra S., and Barbara M. LoFrisco. 2012. "How Do Career Centers Use Social Networking Sites?" *The Career Development Quarterly* 60: 263–72.

Osborn, Debra S., Julia Kronholz, J. Tyler Finklea, and Anastasia M. Cantonis. 2014. "Technology-Savvy Career Counselling." *Canadian Psychology* 55(4): 258–65.

Pace University Study Abroad. 2019. Located at: https://www.instagram.com/pacestudyabroad/. Last accessed: 8 July 2019.

Packard, Becky W. 2003. "Web-based Mentoring: Challenging Traditional Models to Increase Women's Access." *Mentoring and Tutoring* 11: 44–52.

Pascarella, Ernest, and Patrick Terenzini. 2005. *How College Affects Students: A Third Decade of Research (Vol. 2)*. San Francisco: Jossey-Bass.

———. 1991. *How College Affects Students: Findings and Insights from Twenty Years of Research*. San Francisco: Jossey-Bass.

Pennsylvania State University. 2015. *Twitter Chat: Undergraduate Admissions*. Located at: https://twitter.com/PSUWorldCampus. Last accessed: 7 August 2019.

Perigo, Donald J., and M. Lee Upcraft. 1989. "Orientation Programs." In *The Freshman Year Experience*, edited by M. Lee Upcraft, John Gardner, and Associates. San Francisco: Jossey-Bass.

Phoenix College. 2018. Located at: https://news.phoenixcollege.edu/bytes/2016/11/08/1-new-social-media-tool-mentoring-students. Last accessed: 8 July 2019.

Ponisciak, Tim. n.d. "Engaging Alumni on Social Media: What Works." Located at: https://www.academicimpressions.com/sites/default/files/engaging-alumni-social-media.pdf. Last accessed: 8 July 2019.

Popper, Ben. 2017. "The Empathy Layer." *The Verge*, 2 March. Located at: https://www.theverge.com/2017/3/2/14764620/koko-social-network-mental-health-depression-app-kik. Last accessed: 8 July 2019.

Powell, John, Michael Pander, and Robert Nielsen. 1994. *Campus Security and Law Enforcement*. Newton, MA: Butterworth-Heinemann.

Princeton University Career Services. 2019. Located at: https://twitter.com/princetoncareer. Last accessed: 28 July 2019.

Ra, Chaelin K., Junhan Cho, and Matthew D. Stone. 2018. "Association of Digital Media Use with Subsequent Symptoms of Attention-Deficit/Hyperactivity Disorder Among Adolescents." *JAMA* 320(3): 255–63.

Ragins, Belle R., and John L. Cotton. 1991. "Easier Said Than Done: Gender Differences in Perceived Barriers to Gaining a Mentor." *Human Relations* 42: 1–22.

Redmond, Sonjia P. 1990. "Mentoring and Cultural Diversity in Academic Settings." *American Behavioral Scientist* 34: 188–200.

Rodriguez, Julia E. 2011. "Social Media Use in Higher Education: Key Areas to Consider for Educators." *Journal of Online Learning and Teaching* 7 (4 December): 539–51.

Rogers, Gil. 2015. "How Students (Really) Decide: Class of 2015." *Journal of College Admission* 228: 42–43.

———. 2014. "How Students (Really) Decide." *Journal of College Admission* 223: 49–50.

Ross, Megan. 2017. "Harvard Rescinds Acceptances for at Least Ten Students for Obscene Memes." *The Harvard Crimson*, 5 June. Located at: https://www.thecrimson.com/article/2017/6/5/2021-offers-rescinded-memes/. Last accessed: 8 July 2019.

Russell, Joyce, and Danielle M. Adams. 1997. "The Changing Nature of Mentoring in Organizations: An Introduction to the Special Issue on Mentoring in Organizations." *Journal of Vocational Behavior* 51: 1–14.

Sampson, James P. Jr., and Debra S. Osborn. 2014. "Using Information and Communication Technology in Delivering Career Interventions." In *APA Handbook of Career Intervention: Vol. 2. Applications*, edited by Paul J. Hartung, Mark L. Savickas, and W. Bruce Walsh. Washington, DC: American Psychological Association.

Samuel, Alexandra. 2016. "Psychographics Are Just as Important for Marketers as Demographics." *Harvard Business Review*, 11 March. Located at: https://hbr.org/2016/03/psychographics-are-just-as-important-for-marketers-as-demographics. Last accessed: 8 July 2019.

Sands, Roberta G., L. Alayne Parson, and Josann Duane. 1992. "Faculty-Faculty Mentoring and Discrimination: Perceptions Among Asian, Asian American, and Pacific Island Faculty." *Equity and Excellence* 25: 124–29.

San Jose State University Twitter Page. 2016. Located at: https://twitter.com/SJSU/status/765232029520781312. Last accessed: 8 July 2019.

Saw, Grace, Wendy Abbott, Jessie Donaghey, and Carolyn McDonald. 2012. "Social Media for International Students: It's Not All About Facebook." *Proceedings of the IATUL Conferences*. Paper 19. Located at: https://docs.lib.purdue.edu/cgi/viewcontent.cgi?referer=https://www.google.com/&httpsredir=1&article=1109&context=iatul. Last accessed: 8 July 2019.

Schildkraut, Jaclyn, Joseph M. McKenna, and H. Jaymi Elsass. 2016. "Understanding Crisis Communications: Examining Students' Perceptions About Campus Notification Systems." *Security Journal* 30(2): 605–20.

Schlossberg, Nancy K., Ann Q. Lynch, and Arthur W. Chickering. 1989. *Improving Higher Education Environments for Adults: Responsive Programs and Services from Entry to Departure*. San Francisco: Jossey-Bass.

Selingo, Jeffrey. 2017a. "How Colleges Use Big Data to Target the Students They Want." *The Atlantic*. Located at: https://www.theatlantic.com/education/archive/2017/04/how-colleges-find-their-students/522516/. Last accessed: 8 July 2019.

———. 2017b. "Colleges' Endless Pursuit of Students." *The Atlantic*, 10 April. Located at: https://www.theatlantic.com/education/archive/2017/04/the-business-of-college-marketing/522399/. Last accessed: 8 July 2019.

Shaffer, Leigh S., Jacqueline M. Zalewski, and John Leveille. 2010. "The Professionalization of Academic Advising: Where Are We in 2010?" *National Academic Advising Association Journal* 30: 66–77.

Shaw, Jen Day, and Sarah B. Westfall. 2015. "Behavior Intervention and Case Management." In *College in the Crosshairs*, edited by Brandi Hephner LaBanc and Brian O. Hemphill. Sterling, VA: Stylus.

BIBLIOGRAPHY

Sin, Sei-Ching Joanna, and Kyung-Sun Kim. 2013. "International Students' Everyday Life Information Seeking: The Informational Value of Social Networking Sites." *Library & Information Science Research* 35: 107–16.

Single, Peg B. 2004. "Expanding Our Use of Mentoring: Reflection and Reaction." Paper presented at the Annual Meeting of the American Educational Research Association. San Diego, CA.

Single, Peg B., and Richard M. Single. 2005. "E-mentoring for Social Equity: Review of Research to Inform Program Development." *Mentoring and Tutoring* 13: 301–20.

Skari, Lisa Ann. 2014. "Community College Alumni: Predicting Who Gives." *Community College Review* 42(1): 23–40.

Sleek, Scott. 2014. "The Psychological Toll of the Smartphone." Located at: https://www.psychologicalscience.org/observer/the-psychological-toll-of-the-smartphone. Last accessed: 8 July 2019.

Smith, Julia B., Timothy Walter, and George Hoey. 1992. "Support Programs and Student Self-Efficacy: Do First-Year Students Know When They Need Help?" *Journal of the Freshman Year Experience* 4: 41–67.

Sproull, Lee, and Sara Kiesler. 1992. *Connections: New Ways of Working in the Networked Organization*. Cambridge, MA: MIT Press.

Steele, Claude M. 1997. "A Threat in the Air: How Stereotypes Shape Intellectual Identity and Performance." *American Psychologist* 52: 613–29.

Steinberg, Jacques. 2010. "That Facebook Welcome to the Class of 2015? Not So Fast, Colleges Say." Located at: https://thechoice.blogs.nytimes.com/2010/12/07/freshmen-faceboo/?partner=rss&emc=rss. Last accessed: 8 July 2019.

Steinfield, Charles, Nicole Ellison, and Cliff Lampe. 2008. "Social Capital, Self-Esteem, and Use of Online Social Network Sites: A Longitudinal Analysis." *Journal of Applied Developmental Psychology* 29(6): 434–45.

Stephens, Keri K., Ashley K. Barrett, and Michael J. Mahometa. 2013. "Organizational Communication in Emergencies: Using Multiple Channels and Sources to Combat Noise and Capture Attention." *Human Communication Research* 39(2): 230–51.

Stephens-Davidowitz, Seth. 2017. "Don't Let Facebook Make You Miserable." *New York Times*, 6 May. Located at: https://www.nytimes.com/2017/05/06/opinion/sunday/dont-let-facebook-make-you-miserable.html. Last accessed: 8 July 2019.

Strom, Ralph J. 1950. *The Disabled College Veteran of World War II*. Washington, DC: American Council on Education.

Strong, Thomas S. 1994. "The Technology and Information Explosion." In *Technology in Student Affairs: Issues, Applications, and Trends*, edited by John L. Baier and Thomas S. Strong. Lanham, MD: University Press of America.

Student Press Law Center. 2017. "News Release: Supreme Court Urged to Restrict Colleges' Authority to Discipline Off-campus Social Media Speech." Located at: http://www.splc.org/article/2017/03/news-release-supreme-court-urged-to-restrict-colleges-authority-to-discipline-off-campus-social-media-speech. Last accessed: 8 July 2019.

Terenzini, Patrick T. 1986. "Retention Research: Academic and Social Fit." Paper presented at the annual meeting of the Southern Regional Office of the College Entrance Examination Board. New Orleans, LA.

Tess, Paul A. 2013. "The Role of Social Media in Higher Education Classes (Real and Virtual)—A Literature Review." *Computers in Human Behavior* 29: A60–68.

Texas A&M University Department of International Studies. 2019. Located at: https://twitter.com/TAMUINTS. Last accessed: 7 August 2019.

Texas A&M University Office of International Student Services. 2013. Located at: https://www.facebook.com/events/541951322506461/. Last accessed: 8 July 2019.

Tinker v. Des Moines 393 U.S. 503 (1969).

Tinto, Vincent. 1987. *Leaving College: Rethinking the Causes and Cures for Student Attrition*. Chicago: University of Chicago Press.

———. 1975. "Dropout from Higher Education: A Theoretical Synthesis of Recent Research." *Review of Educational Research* 45: 89–125.

Titley, Robert, and Bonnie Titley. 1980. "Initial Choice of College Major: Are Only the 'Undecided' Undecided?" *Journal of College Student Personnel* 21: 293–98.

Turner, Caroline, and Judith R. Thompson. 1993. "Socializing Women Doctoral Students: Minority and Majority Experiences." *Review of Higher Education* 16: 355–70.

Twombly, Susan, Mark Salisbury, Shannon Tumanut, and Paul Klute. 2012. *Study Abroad in the New Global Century: Renewing the Promise, Refining the Purpose.* San Francisco, CA: Wiley Subscription Services.

Underwood, Zach, and Ryan Underwood. 2015. "Technology's Evolving Role in Prescriptive and Developmental Advising." *Academic Advising Today* 38(4). Located at: http://www.nacada.ksu.edu/Resources/Academic-Advising-Today/View-Articles/Technologys-Evolving-Role-in-Prescriptive-and-Developmental-Advising.aspx. Last accessed: 8 July 2019.

University of Buffalo Pre-Law Advising Blog. 2019. Located at: http://prelaw.buffalo.edu/blog/. Last accessed: 8 July 2019.

University of Iowa. 2019 Twitter Page. Located at: https://twitter.com/uiowa/status/1100446244114190337. Last accessed: 8 July 2019.

University of Michigan Alumni Association. 2019. Located at: https://www.facebook.com/michiganalumni/. Last accessed: 8 July 2019.

University of Minnesota. 2019. "Orientation & Transition Experiences." Located at: https://www.ofyp.umn.edu/more/communication-publications/social-media. Last accessed: 8 July 2019.

University of Minnesota Duluth Study Abroad. 2019. Located at: https://www.linkedin.com/in/umdstudyabroad/detail/recent-activity/posts/. Last accessed: 9 July 2019.

University of New Hampshire Social Media. 2016. "UNH Move-In Weekend." Located at: https://medium.com/@UNHSocial/unh-move-in-weekend-a3b119309854. Last accessed: 9 July 2019.

University of North Carolina Wilmington Study Abroad. 2019. Located at: https://twitter.com/search?q=social%20media%20study%20abroad&src=typd. Last accessed: 9 July 2019.

University of Oxford Alumni. 2019. Located at: https://www.facebook.com/oxfordalumni/. Last accessed: 9 July 2019.

University of Pennsylvania Career Services. 2019. Located at: https://www.vpul.upenn.edu/careerservices/. Last accessed: 28 July 2019.

University of Salford. 2017. "Tinder 'Recruitment' Campaign Wins National Award." Located at: https://www.salford.ac.uk/news/articles/tinder-recruitment-campaign-win-national-award. Last accessed: 9 July 2019.

University of Washington. 2019. *National First-Generation College Celebration Social Media Toolkit.* Located at: http://www.washington.edu/diversity/national-first-gen-day/toolkit/. Last accessed: 9 July 2019.

University of Wisconsin International Student Services. 2019. Located at: https://www.facebook.com/pg/ISSatUW/events/?ref=page_internal. Last accessed: 9 July 2019.

Upcraft, M. Lee, Joni E. Finney, and Peter Garland. 1984. "Orientation: A Context." In *Orienting Students to College*, edited by M. Lee Upcraft. San Francisco: Jossey-Bass.

Waite, Brandon, and Darren Wheeler. 2016. *Understanding and Using Social Media on College Campuses: A Practical Guide for Higher Education Professionals.* New York: Rowman & Littlefield.

Walker, Suzanne C., and Deborah J. Taub. 2001. "Variables Correlated with Satisfaction with a Mentoring Relationship in First-Year College Students and Their Mentors." *Journal of the First Year Experience and Students in Transition* 13: 47–67.

Watson, Linda. 2014. "Security Assessments and Prevention for K-12 Schools." In *The Handbook for School Safety and Security*, edited by Lawrence J. Fennelly and Marianna A. Perry. Oxford, UK: Elsevier.

Webb, Charles H., ed. 1989. *Handbook for Alumni Administration.* New York: Macmillan.

Weinreich, Nedra K. 2010. *Hands-On Social Marketing: A Step-by-Step Guide to Designing Change for Good.* Thousand Oaks, CA: Sage.

West, Delia S. et al. 2016. "A Technology-Mediated Behavioral Weight Gain Prevention Intervention for College Students: Controlled, Quasi-Experimental Study." *Journal of Medical Internet Research* 18(6): e133.

Whillans, Ashley, Chelsea D. Christie, Sarah Cheung, Alexander H. Jordan, and Frances S. Chen. 2017. "From Misperception to Social Connection: Correlates and Consequences of Overestimating Others' Social Connectedness." *Personality and Social Psychology Bulletin* 43: 1696–711.

Wilcox, Paula, Sandra Winn, and Marylynn Fyvie-Gauld. 2005. "'It Was Nothing to Do with the University, It Was Just the People': The Role of Social Support in the First-Year Experience of Higher Education." *Studies in Higher Education* 30: 707–22.

Wilkes University. 2018. *E-Mentoring*. Located at: https://www.wilkes.edu/campus-life/student-development/leadership-opportunities/e-mentoring/index.aspx. Last accessed: 9 July 2019.

Williams, Samantha Estoesta. 2017. "3 Stellar Student Recruitment Campaigns Using Social Media." *Mad Hatter*, 21 August. Located at: https://www.madhattertech.ca/chatter/3-stellar-student-recruitment-campaigns-using-social-media. Lasted Accessed: 9 July 2019.

Winn, Zach. 2016a. "Tackling Social Media Monitoring's Liability, Clery Compliance Questions." Located at: https://www.campussafetymagazine.com/safety/tackling_social_media_monitorings_liability_clery_compliance_questions/. Last accessed: 9 July 2019.

———. 2016b. "Countering Potential Campus Threats with Social Media Monitoring." Located at: https://www.campussafetymagazine.com/safety/countering_potential_threats_with_social_media_monitoring/. Last accessed: 9 July 2019.

Winston, Hannah. 2013. "Looking to Make Connections, Alumni Log On to LinkedIn." *Chronicle of Higher Education* 60(9): 16–17.

Winston, Roger B., Steven Ender, and Theodore K. Miller, eds. 1984. *Developmental Academic Advising*. San Francisco: Jossey-Bass.

Wood, Eileen et al. 2011. "Examining the Impact of Off-Task Multi-Tasking with Technology on Real-Time Classroom Learning." *Computers & Education* 58: 365–74.

Wyckoff, Susan C. 1999. "The Academic Advising Process in Higher Education: History, Research, and Improvement." *Recruitment and Retention in Higher Education* 13: 1–3.

Zhang, Naijan, ed. 2011. *Rentz's Student Affairs Practice in Higher Education*. Springfield, IL: Charles C. Thomas.

Zullig, Keith, Daniel Teoli, and Robert Valois. 2011. "Evaluating a Brief Measure of Social Self-Efficacy Among U.S. Adolescents." *Psychological Reports* 109; 907–20.

ABOUT THE AUTHORS

Brandon C. Waite earned his PhD in political science from the University of Tennessee in 2008, and he is an associate professor of political science at Ball State University. His teaching, research, and service activities focus on new media technologies. Dr. Waite teaches undergraduate and graduate courses in media, public administration, public policy, and American national government. His research deals with the use of online technologies for campaigning and organizational communication. His writings have appeared in numerous books and academic journals.

As an emerging media faculty fellow with BSU's Center for Media Design, Dr. Waite has also directed several applied research projects involving new media technologies. One involved a collaboration with CSPAN on the design of an interactive television news application that could be used by viewers during televised hearings. In another project, he helped design and test an application for the Apple iPad that aggregated "tagged" content from a number of online sources relevant to the 2012 presidential contest and allowed users to immediately access relevant data while watching televised presidential debates.

Dr. Waite is the coauthor of *Understanding and Using Social Media on College Campuses: A Practical Guide for Higher Education Professionals* (Rowman & Littlefield, 2016). He regularly gives presentations about social media to nonprofit organizations and candidates for office on behalf of the Bowen Center for Public Affairs and is the coadministrator of the BSU Political Science Department Facebook page.

Darren A. Wheeler earned his PhD in political science from Miami University in Oxford, Ohio, in 2004 with a specialization in judicial politics. He is a professor and chairperson of the Political Science Department at Ball State University, where he has taught since 2009. He was previously at Northwest College in Wyoming and the University of North Florida. Dr. Wheeler's teaching and research interests include judicial politics, the American presidency, terrorism and homeland security, and social media.

Along with coauthoring *Understanding and Using Social Media on College Campuses: A Practical Guide for Higher Education Professionals* (Rowman & Littlefield, 2016), Dr. Wheeler is the author of *Presidential Power in Action: Implementing Supreme Court Detainee Decisions* (2008) and *Congress and the War on Terror* (2018). He has also written numerous articles on topics such as the implementation of judicial decisions, presidential power, civil liberties and the War on Terror, and the use of social media in administrative settings. Dr. Wheeler has been teaching online classes at colleges and universities for more than fifteen years and is the coadministrator of the BSU Political Science Department Facebook page.

www.ingramcontent.com/pod-product-compliance
Lightning Source LLC
Chambersburg PA
CBHW020742230426
43665CB00009B/525